I0820108

WILD
EARTH

Journeys of discovery to the untouched treasures of our world

WILD EARTH

BECAUSE WE ARE PART OF THIS EARTH

This magnificent book, *Wild Earth*, is an ode to the diversity of nature on our planet – both in the sea and on land – encompassing both geological and biological diversity. Through around 170 selected locations across all five continents, the photographs and descriptions reveal the fascinating variety of our Earth.

Today, humanity occupies a unique position among the approximately 2.5 million known species recorded in natural history museums. We are deeply animal in our nature: we share the same thyroid gland as a trout; like all mammals, we possess a brain, blood, kidneys, a liver and a heart. Our bodies consist of water (80 percent of our brain and 75 percent of our body at birth), as well as salts and cells. Yet, we tend to forget this. Our internal physiology tells the story of the transition from sea to land half a billion years ago. And yet, today, humans behave like cruel and irresponsible destroyers of ecosystems – polluters, developers and exploiters without measure. Through our economic activities, we even have the power to profoundly and permanently alter the climate.

How can we seriously assume that no severe health crises will arise if we continue to harm our environment in this way? We breathe air, drink water and constantly consume elements of the biodiversity that surrounds us. That is why we must take far greater care of it.

This book can help us do just that by opening our eyes to the wonders of planet Earth – the very wonders that all astronauts have seen when looking through a small porthole at our entire planet, spinning in the darkness of interstellar space. While humanity is essentially animal in its biological makeup, it is also more than that. It has embraced what Paul Crutzen, in 2001, called the Anthropocene: a stance of destructive dominance over our environment, combined with an explosive demographic expansion that has quadrupled the human population in less than a century.

For this reason, a work like this is indispensable. It should serve as a powerful, collective wake-up call, urging us to respect other forms of life and to take joy in sharing and appreciating the breathtaking nature that surrounds us – depicted here so beautifully. The Earth was formed 4.6 billion years ago, life emerged around four billion years ago, then transitioned from water to land approximately half a billion years ago, and humans have only existed for 400,000 years. Life began in the primordial ocean as isolated cells, which much later ventured onto land, but always retained a fundamental principle: once out of water, always within the body.

This book is filled with stunning photographs of water – whether salty, brackish (like our blood) or fresh water, which we can drink. Without water, the Earth would be nothing but deserts – and indeed, some of these are featured in this book. Life endures there, but with great difficulty and only through extraordinary adaptations. In contrast, where water is abundant, such as in tropical rainforests or coral reefs, we find the highest density of species – sometimes exceeding 30,000 different species per square kilometre.

The ancient mineral world (wonderfully captured in many of the locations selected here) was significantly shaped by the emergence of life and the production of oxygen more than three billion years ago. Many of the 5,200 minerals known today would not exist without life. Minerals and life have interwoven through the process of biomineralization (in the form of skeletons, eggshells, seashells and more).

Scientific research requires precision across all disciplines, but we must also convey passion, participation, love and a sense of wonder for this Earth that sustains us. This is the key to ensuring that a message truly resonates. May this book inspire in each of us a genuine awareness of the consequences of our actions, encouraging us to significantly reduce our short-sightedness, arrogance and greed!

Gilles Boeuf
Emeritus Professor at Sorbonne University,
Visiting Professor at the Collège de France,
Former Chairman of the Muséum national d'Histoire naturelle,
Chairman of the CEEBIOS Research Institute

EUROPE 10

Iceland
1 Háifoss 12
2 Strokkur 12
3 Gullfoss 12
4 Vatnajökull National Park 14

Norway
5 Lofoten 16
6 Geirangerfjord 18
7 Hallingskarvet National Park 20

Sweden
8 Sarek National Park 22

Denmark
9 Faroe Islands 24

Finland
10 Oulanka National Park 26

Ireland
11 Iveragh Peninsula 28

Great Britain and Northern Ireland
12 Giant's Causeway 30
13 Glen Coe 32
14 Peak District National Park 34
15 Jurassic Coast 36

France
16 Islands and Sea of Iroise 38
17 Mont Blanc Massif 40
18 Verdon Regional Natural Park 42
19 Calanques National Park 44

Germany
20 Schleswig-Holstein Wadden Sea National Park 46
21 Saxon Switzerland National Park 48
22 Berchtesgaden National Park 50
23 Watzmann 50

Switzerland
24 Matterhorn 52

Austria
25 High Tauern National Park 54

Poland
26 Tatra National Park 56

Portugal
27 Sintra-Cascais Natural Park 58
28 Praia da Ursa 58
29 Algarve Coast 60

Spain
30 Costa Quebrada 62
31 Bardenas Reales 64
32 Doñana National Park 66
33 Teide National Park 68

Italy
34 Sexten Dolomites 70
35 Gran Paradiso National Park 72
36 Monti Sibillini National Park 74
37 Cinque Terre National Park 76

Slovenia
38 Julian Alps 78

Croatia
39 Plitvice Lakes National Park 80

Montenegro
40 Durmitor National Park 82

Romania
41 Bucegi Natural Park 84

Bulgaria
42 Pirin National Park 86

Greece
43 Metéora 88
44 Zakynthos Marine National Park 90

AFRICA 92

Morocco
45 High Atlas 94

Tunisia
46 Sidi Toui National Park 96

Algeria
47 Tassili n'Ajjer National Park 98

Libya
48 Erg Ubari and Umm al-Maa 100

Egypt
49 Ras Mohammed National Park 102

Ethiopia
50 Simien Mountains National Park 104

Senegal
51 Niokolo-Koba National Park 106

Niger · Burkina Faso · Benin
52 W-Arly-Pendjari 108

Chad
53 Ennedi Massif 110

Nigeria
54 Chad Basin National Park 112

Cameroon
55 Campo-Ma'an National Park 114

Central African Republic
56 André-Félix National Park 116

Democratic Republic of the Congo
57 Maiko National Park 118

Uganda
58 Rwenzori Mountains National Park 120

Kenya
59 Mount Kenya National Park 122
60 Maasai Mara National Reserve 124

Tanzania
61 Kilimanjaro National Park 126
62 Ngorongoro Conservation Area 128
63 Serengeti National Park 130

South Africa · Angola · Namibia
64 Namib Desert 132

Namibia
65 Etosha National Park 134

Zambia
66 Mosi-oa-Tunya National Park 136

Malawi
67 Lake Chilwa Wetland Biosphere Reserve 138

South Africa
68 The Drakensberg 140
69 Tugela Falls and Tugela Canyon 140
70 Karoo National Park 142
71 Kruger National Park 144

Botswana
72 Okavango Delta 146

Seychelles
73 La Digue 148
74 Cocos Island Marine National Park 148

La Réunion
75 Réunion National Park 150

THE AMERICAS 152

Canada
76 Pacific Rim National Park 154
77 Jasper National Park 156
78 Forillon National Park 158

USA
79 Denali National Park 160
80 Yosemite National Park 162
81 Death Valley National Park 164
82 Devil's Golf Course 164
83 Mesquite Flat Sand Dunes 164
84 Artist's Palette 164
85 Golden Canyon 164
86 Yellowstone National Park 166
87 Grand Canyon of the Yellowstone 166
88 Upper Geyser Basin 166
89 Lower Geyser Basin 166
90 Old Faithful 166
91 Canyonlands National Park 168
92 Island in the Sky 168
93 White Rim 168
94 Dead Horse Point State Park 168
95 The Needles 168
96 Angel Arch 168
97 Bryce Canyon National Park 170
98 Grand Canyon National Park 172
99 Sequoia National Park 174
100 Everglades National Park 176
101 Hawai'i Volcanoes National Park 178

Mexico
102 Sian Ka'an Biosphere Reserve 180

Guadeloupe
103 Guadeloupe National Park 182

Honduras
104 Río Plátano Biosphere Reserve 184

Costa Rica
105 Cordillera Volcánica Central Biosphere Reserve 186
106 Poás 186
107 Irazú 186

Venezuela
108 Canaima National Park 188
109 Angel Falls 188

Brazil
110 Amazon and Amazon Rainforest 190
111 Chapada dos Veadeiros National Park 192
112 Iguaçu National Park 194

Colombia
113 Tayrona National Park 196

Ecuador
114 Galápagos National Park 198

Peru
115 Cordillera Blanca 200

Bolivia
116 Altiplano 202
117 Eduardo Avaroa Andean Fauna National Reserve 204

Chile
118 Torres del Paine National Park 206
119 Cerro Paine Grande 206

Argentina
120 Quebrada de Humahuaca 208
121 Tierra del Fuego National Park 210

Antarctica
122 Antarctic Peninsula 212

ASIA 214

Azerbaijan
123 Mud Volcanoes of Qobustan 216

Turkey
124 Göreme National Park 218

Israel
125 Dead Sea 220

Jordan
126 Wadi Rum Nature Reserve 222

Tajikistan
127 Pamir Mountains 224

Mongolia
128 Gobi Gurvansaikhan National Park 226

China
129 Tian Shan 228
130 Wulong Karst 230
131 Wulingyuan Scenic and Historic Interest Area 232
132 Zhangye Danxia Geopark 234

South Korea
133 Gyeongju National Park 236

Japan
134 Shiretoko National Park 238
135 Fuji-Hakone-Izu National Park 240
136 Sobo, Katamuki and Okue Biosphere Reserve 242

Pakistan
137 Karakorum 244

Nepal
138 Sagarmatha National Park 246
139 Chitwan National Park 248

India
140 Hemis National Park 250
141 Ranthambore National Park 252

Maldives
142 Baa Atoll Biosphere Reserve 254

Sri Lanka
143 Yala National Park 256

Thailand
144 Sam Phan Bok 258
145 Mu Ko Similan National Park 260
146 Ao Phang-Nga National Park 262

Vietnam
147 Ban Gioc-Detian Falls 264
148 Halong Bay 266

Malaysia
149 Niah National Park 268
150 Taman Negara National Park 270

Philippines
151 Mayon Volcano Natural Park 272
152 Mayon 272

Indonesia
153 Gunung Leuser National Park 274
154 Bromo Tengger Semeru National Park 276
155 Java's Fire Mountains 276

AUSTRALIA & OCEANIA 278

Australia
156 Great Barrier Reef 280
157 Wet Tropics of Queensland 282
158 Kakadu National Park 284
159 Uluru-Kata Tjuta National Park 286
160 Uluru 286
161 Lake Eyre National Park 288

New Zealand
162 Tongariro National Park 290
163 Fiordland National Park 292
164 Campbell Island 294

Palau
165 Southern Lagoon of the Chelbacheb Islands 296

Solomon Islands
166 Marovo Lagoon 298

French Polynesia
167 Rangiroa 300
168 Lagoon of Bora Bora 302

CONTENTS

OVERVIEW MAPS

ARCTIC OCEAN
NORTH AMERICA
ATLANTIC OCEAN
EUROPE
AFRICA
PACIFIC OCEAN
SOUTH AMERICA
SOUTHERN OCEAN
TROPIC OF CANCER
EQUATOR
TROPIC OF CAPRICORN
1 2 3 4 9
76 77 78 79
80 81 82 83 84 85 86 87 88 89 90 91 92 93 94 95 96 97 98 99
100 101 102 103 104 105 106 107 108 109 110 111 112 113 114 115 116 117 118 119 120 121 122
167 168

EUROPE

LOCATION Bláskógabyggð, southern Iceland, near the Great Geysir in Haukadalur
HEIGHT 25–35 metres

Strokkur

Ochre-coloured rock, porous, rust-red and green-spotted with minerals, and in the middle, a modestly rippling puddle: Strokkur. The main attraction in Haukadalur lies dormant, but only for a short while, as the geyser erupts towards the sky with fascinating regularity. Its tension builds slowly. If you look closely, you can see a pulsation in the water and the swelling of a blue-glowing bubble. As the water retreats into the fissure, the eruption is imminent. Strokkur shoots its fountain an impressive 30 metres high and it does so in intervals of just a few minutes. Geysers in geothermal areas are formed when water gets trapped in fissures in the earth, which then explode due to the formation of steam.

LOCATION Between Þjórsárdalur and Fossárdalur, southern Iceland
WIDTH 12 metres
RIVER Fossá í Þjórsárdal

Háifoss
ICELAND

This waterfall lies north of Hekla and is the third-highest in Iceland, after Morsárfoss and Glymur. The Fossá River plunges 122 metres down over a steep drop. Not far from Háifoss, there is another waterfall, Granni ("Neighbour"), which also falls into the same gorge and is equally stunning. If you are fortunate enough to witness these waterfalls in the sunshine, you will see a beautiful rainbow in the mist of the water. You can reach Háifoss either via a trail only passable with a 4x4 vehicle or by hiking. The hike starts at the Stöng archaeological site and leads without any marked trail through the Fossá Valley, which is partly bordered by colourful rhyolite mountains. After about three hours, you'll reach the upper part of the waterfall. A narrow, steep path descends from there to the base of Háifoss, leading to a green oasis.

LOCATION Between Hrunamannahreppur and Bláskógabyggð, southern Iceland, near Haukadalur
WIDTH 229 metres
RIVER Hvítá

Gullfoss

The "Golden Waterfall", Gullfoss is one of the most beautiful and visited waterfalls in Iceland. The Hvítá ("White River") flows over two separate cascades, falling a total of about 30 metres into a narrow gorge, several kilometres long. In the summer, when most visitors come, the Hvítá carries more than 100 cubic metres of water per second, making Gullfoss an impressive spectacle. The fact that the waterfall, which is now state-owned, was not sacrificed for energy production and still flows as a small stream into the gorge is largely thanks to the courage of Sigriður Tómasdóttir, a local farmer's daughter, who advocated for the preservation of Gullfoss. A monument in her honour can be found nearby.

LOCATION Norðurland eystra, Austurland and Suðurland regions
SIZE 14,200km²
ESTABLISHED 2008
UNESCO World Heritage Site since 2019
vatnajokulsthjodgardur.is

Vatnajökull National Park
ICELAND

Established in 2008, the Vatnajökull National Park covers over 12,000 square kilometres, making it the largest national park in Europe. It encompasses the entire Vatnajökull glacier, the former independent national parks of Skaftafell and Jökulsárgljúfur, as well as the volcanic massifs of Askja and Herðubreið. Unlike many other glaciers in Iceland, Vatnajökull did not form during the last ice age, but rather about 2,500 years ago. It expanded significantly during the so-called Little Ice Age, which lasted from the fifteenth century to the end of the nineteenth century. Since then, the glacier has been shrinking. The northern part of Vatnajökull is located in the highlands, accessible only by rough 4x4 tracks, while the southern edge of the glacier runs along the Ring Road for much of its length. The ice often extends nearly to the coast, with the Ring Road winding through a narrow strip of ice-free land. From Kirkjubæjarklaustur in the west to beyond Höfn in the east, travellers pass through some of the most fascinating landscapes of Iceland, including the vast Skeiðarársandur sand plains. Short detours lead to glacier tongues and glacial lakes dotted with icebergs. However, the true grandeur of this ice giant is only truly realized when climbing one of its peaks, where you can gaze at an endless, sparkling ice expanse stretching to the horizon.

The largest national park in Iceland is renowned for its unique mix of glaciers and volcanoes, lush meadows and rugged rocks, as well as impressive waterfalls and hot springs. During the summer, parts of the Vatnajökull National Park serve as breeding grounds for several bird species, especially around the lagoons, where Arctic terns nest. As these birds nest on the ground, their eggs are often at risk from unaware hikers.

LOCATION These 80 islands lie north of the Arctic Circle and are part of Nordland Province
SIZE 1,227km²
infolofoten.no

Lofoten
NORWAY

Often referred to as the "Alps of the Arctic", the magical-seeming landscape of the Lofoten Islands resembles a Swiss mountain range, except with its feet submerged in the sea. This long archipelago is named after the Viking name for a single island: Vestvågøy, originally "Lófóten", meaning "lynx foot" as its outline is said to resemble the shape of a lynx paw. Today, the major islands of Lofoten are connected by bridges or tunnels. Situated 100 kilometres north of the Arctic Circle, the islands experience long winter nights, but the Gulf Stream ensures a relatively mild climate. Fishermen have lived here for around 6,000 years, as evidenced by the widespread stockfish racks and traditional rorbu huts. In recent times, tourism has become one of the major sources of income alongside fishing.

Lofoten captivates with its rugged cliffs, white sandy beaches, meandering rivers and open sea. The best views can be had from above, such as from the summit of Offersøykammen. Dramatic cloud formations sweep over the jagged, sometimes snow-covered peaks of Vestvågøy's alpine mountain range, with steep cliffs rising up to 1,000 metres from the sea.

LOCATION About 200 kilometres northeast of Bergen and roughly 280 kilometres northwest of Oslo, in the province of Møre og Romsdal

SIZE 15km^2

UNESCO World Heritage Site since 2005

Geirangerfjord
NORWAY

The Geirangerfjord, one of the most beautiful landscapes on Earth, has been a UNESCO World Heritage Site since 2005. It is the innermost branch of the 120-kilometre-long Storfjord, which is visited annually by more than 150 cruise ships from around the world. From a ship, you can view the famous waterfalls: "The Seven Sisters", "The Suitor" and "The Bridal Veil". In the summer, Hurtigruten ships also dock in the small village of Geiranger, with a population of just 250, located at the end of the fjord. The Ørneveien (Eagle Road), a winding mountain road leading from Geirangerfjord to the northern Norddalsfjord, is one of the most breathtaking mountain roads in Scandinavia, featuring numerous hairpin turns and viewpoints, making it a highlight for many tourists. The most spectacular viewpoint, however, is only accessible on foot: Flydalshornet, which rises 1,112 metres directly above the fjord.

The Geirangerfjord is considered the jewel among Norwegian fjords, with its characteristic S-shape and waterfalls cascading from the mountainsides, such as the "Seven Sisters". Abandoned mountain farms can be found in the steep hills of the fjord. Some of these have been restored and now serve as important cultural and historical sites.

LOCATION Located within the municipalities of Hol (Buskerud county), and Ulvik and Aurland (Vestland county)
SIZE 450km²
ESTABLISHED 2006

Hallingskarvet National Park
NORWAY

Located 135 kilometres east of Bergen, the Hallingskarvet National Park was established to protect a large mountainous plateau. Spanning 450 square kilometres, the park features mountain peaks as high as 1,933 metres. At an altitude of 1,453 metres, Flakavatnet is the highest lake in Norway. The high plateau is covered with grassy meadows and home to more than 300 species of plants, some of which are Arctic in origin, including alpine gentians, alpine speedwell and the orchid species *Pseudorchis albida*. The park is also home to Arctic-alpine wildlife. Polar foxes, snow hares, moose, large herds of mountain reindeer and golden eagles all find refuge here. The park has several maintained huts and historic shelters along an ancient trade route, providing hikers with places to stay overnight.

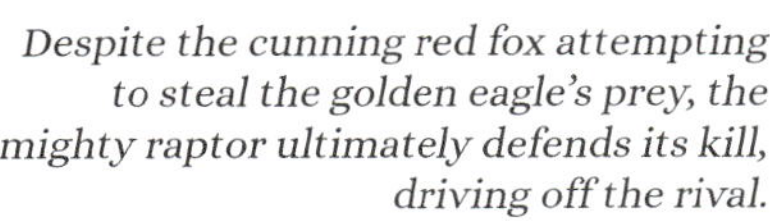

Despite the cunning red fox attempting to steal the golden eagle's prey, the mighty raptor ultimately defends its kill, driving off the rival.

LOCATION Norrbottens län Province, in the municipality of Jokkmokk, Lapland

SIZE 1,970km^2

ESTABLISHED 1909

UNESCO World Heritage Site since 1996

Sarek National Park
SWEDEN

The Sarek National Park offers dramatic and beautiful nature in all its forms, far from any tourism. Viewed from above, one can see the unyielding course of rivers winding through the lush greenery of this landscape. The park is entirely untouched by man-made trails, ensuring an authentic and unspoiled view. Small and large turquoise lakes appear like splashes on the canvas of the land, where nature reigns supreme. This is Lapland's wilderness at its finest and most inaccessible, with vast silent forests and the endless Siberian taiga. Together with other parks, Sarek National Park is part of the UNESCO World Heritage Site "Laponia". It is considered Sweden's most pristine national park and boasts an impressive mix of high plateaus, valleys lined with birch forests and mountain ranges. Almost 100 glaciers lie within this region.

One of Europe's last wild regions, the park is home to animals that brave the harsh conditions. These include alpine ptarmigans, golden plovers, lemmings and the majestic moose.

LOCATION North Atlantic: between the British Isles, Norway and Iceland

SIZE 1,399km²

visitfaroeislands.com/de

Faroe Islands
DENMARK

The Faroe Islands, located in the North Atlantic between the British Isles, Norway and Iceland, consist of 18 islands, almost all of which are permanently inhabited, except for the smaller ones. The archipelago has a volcanic origin, dating back around 60 million years, and is predominantly made of basalt rock. The islands form a pointed triangle: they extend 118 kilometres from Enniberg in the north to Sumbiasteinur in the south and 75 kilometres from Mykinesholmur in the west to Fugloy in the east. No place on the Faroe Islands is more than five kilometres from the sea.

The islands enjoy a relatively mild climate, influenced by the Gulf Stream, and are known for their rapidly changing weather conditions. From the highest mountain, Slættaratindur, visitors can see the entire archipelago and the world's highest sea cliff, at 754 metres, rises vertically from the sea.

One of the most well-known species of the Faroe Islands is the puffin, with its bright orange beak. Due to the isolated location of the islands, this bird is free from larger predators and reptiles.

LOCATION Nordösterbotten Province, within the municipalities of Käylä, Juuma and Hautajärvi
SIZE 290km²
ESTABLISHED 1956
nationalparks.fi/oulankanp

Oulanka National Park
FINLAND

The saying goes that sometimes you can't see the forest for the trees. In Oulanka National Park, in southern Finnish Lapland, you can't see anything but forest. An incredible two-thirds of Finland's land area is covered by forest, and nowhere is this more impressive than in Oulanka, a rugged, uninhabited world of valleys, canyons and bogs, where lynxes, wolves, wolverines and bears roam. A profound silence envelops the land. It feels as though this forest has always existed, yet at the turn of the twentieth century, a terrible wildfire reduced the entire region to ashes. The forest, therefore, is relatively young and incredibly resilient in the face of harsh winters.

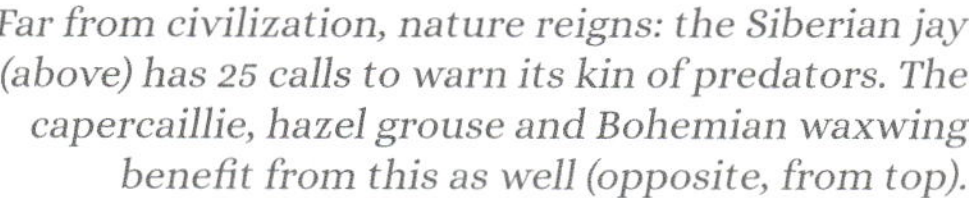

Far from civilization, nature reigns: the Siberian jay (above) has 25 calls to warn its kin of predators. The capercaillie, hazel grouse and Bohemian waxwing benefit from this as well (opposite, from top).

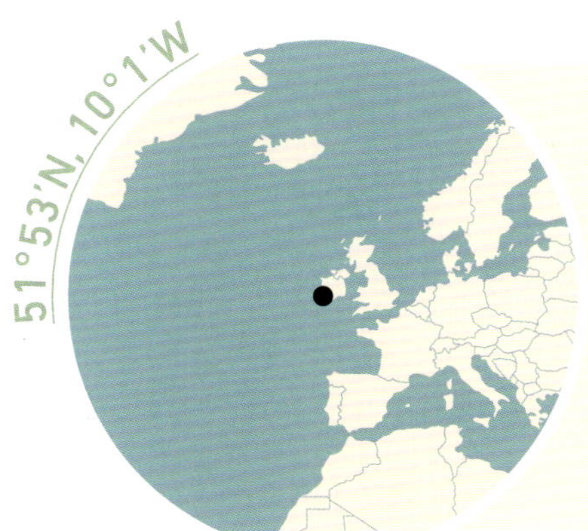

LOCATION County Kerry, in southwest Ireland

SIZE 102km²

Establishment of Killarney National Park: 1932

Iveragh Peninsula
IRELAND

The Iveragh Peninsula in County Kerry is one of the most exciting destinations in Ireland. The area is home to some of Ireland's highest mountains, Killarney National Park, just inland, as well as numerous prehistoric monuments which give a rich insight into the country's history. The peninsula is accessed via the Ring of Kerry, a sweeping road offering stunning, panoramic views. Cyclists will be able to experience the area's raw beauty more easily by exploring the area on the less accessible by-roads. Several ancient ring forts can be found on the peninsula, including Cahergall, a stone fort built in the Iron Age, and Leacanabuaile Fort, the walls of which are over two metres thick, and were built in the ninth or tenth century. Ogham stones can be seen at Cloghanecarhan, also on the peninsula, featuring an ancient script that dates back to around 600 AD.

At Rossbeigh Beach, there is a shipwreck submerged in the sand which, with its rib-like planks, resembles a blackened skeleton.

LOCATION Northern coast of County Antrim, east of Bushmills, 80 kilometres from Belfast

SIZE 0.7km^2

UNESCO World Heritage Site since 1986

Giant's Causeway
NORTHERN IRELAND

The main attraction of Northern Ireland's Causeway Coast is the Giant's Causeway, which can be reached by a heritage railway from Bushmills. This natural wonder, known as the "Road of the Giant", is steeped in many legends. One such tale tells of the Irish giant Finn MacCool who, challenged by a rival, is said to have built a stone path across the sea to Scotland, where similar basalt formations can be found on the island of Staffa. Scientists offer a more sober explanation for this UNESCO World Heritage Site: they believe it formed about 60 million years ago through crystallization processes when lava from underground eruptions slowly cooled as it flowed into the sea. The result is around 40,000 basalt columns, some reaching up to six metres high, forming a five-kilometre-long promontory.

The Giant's Causeway resembles a massive, man-made staircase. Among the mostly hexagonal basalt columns, there are also stones with four, five, seven or even eight sides.

John D. Sutter travelled around the Irish island in a clockwise direction for CNN and described the Giant's Causeway in this way: "A golf-course green canyon wall slopes into a set of volcanic rock formations that are completely surreal: near-perfect hexagon tubes are stacked next to each other like puzzle pieces".

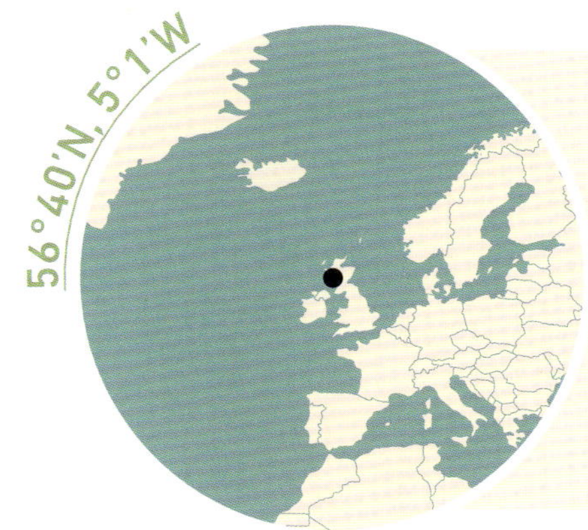

LOCATION In the Scottish Highlands, with nearby Fort William often serving as the starting point for visits

LENGTH 16 kilometres

Glen Coe
SCOTLAND

When the characteristic fog rolls in and the valley of Glen Coe is transformed into a mystical landscape, thoughts may turn to the infamous "Massacre of Glencoe", in which dozens of men, women and children were murdered on a winter's night in 1692. Today, the valley is peaceful and very popular with hikers, who encounter a dreamlike mountain landscape with rugged, snow-capped slopes formed by glacial erosion, waterfalls, lakes, moors and tundra-like vegetation. Glen Coe is situated south of Ben Nevis, the highest mountain in the British Isles at 1,344 metres. However, despite its idyllic location, the rapid and unpredictable weather changes typical of Scotland should not be underestimated.

A pyramid as perfect as a Pharaonic king's tomb: Buachaille Etive Mòr (1,022 metres, depicted in all images) stands like a stone ruler over the valley of Glen Coe. Beloved by winter sports enthusiasts, hikers and climbers alike, the valley has a wild romantic beauty – the James Bond film Skyfall (2012) was shot here.

LOCATION Dark Peak is part of the counties of Greater Manchester and Yorkshire, while the White Peak areas are covered by Staffordshire, Derbyshire and Cheshire

SIZE 1,404km²

ESTABLISHED 1951

peakdistrict.gov.uk

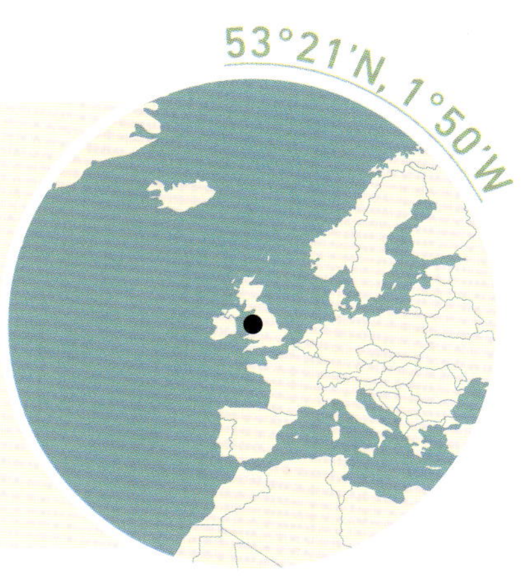

Peak District National Park
ENGLAND

Enclosed by the industrial cities of Manchester, Sheffield and Stoke-on-Trent, the Peak District is England's oldest national park. However, urban dwellers had to fight for their green escape: in 1932, they succeeded in making the mostly privately owned land of the Duke of Devonshire accessible to the public through an illegal mass trespass. Hiking remains the most popular activity in the Peak District, but cyclists, riders, climbers and paragliders also find their playground here. While the northern part, or "Dark Peak", around the 636-metre-high Kinder Scout, is characterized by vast heathlands and moors, solitary peaks and dramatic rock formations, the "White Peak" in the south presents a charming hilly landscape with limestone plateaus, wooded valleys and picturesque villages.

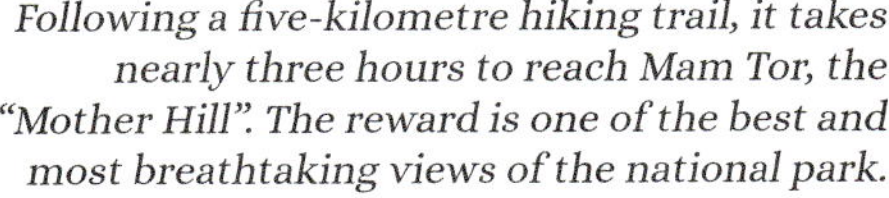

Following a five-kilometre hiking trail, it takes nearly three hours to reach Mam Tor, the "Mother Hill". The reward is one of the best and most breathtaking views of the national park.

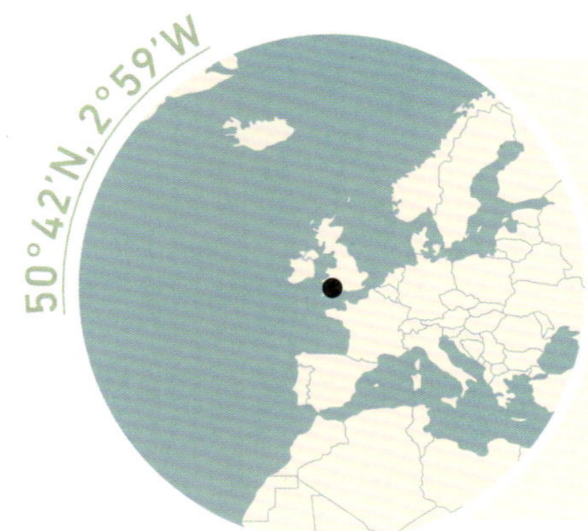

LOCATION In the counties of Dorset and Devon
LENGTH 150 kilometres
UNESCO World Heritage Site since 2001

Jurassic Coast
ENGLAND

Stretching along of the Dorset and East Devon coastline, the Jurassic Coast features spectacular rock formations from the Triassic, Jurassic and Cretaceous periods. These rocks are fossilized witnesses to the evolution and extinction of species, including dinosaurs. In 2000, a dinosaur species unique to this area was discovered, while Mary Anning's discoveries in the early nineteenth century alerted geologists to the site. What appeared at first to resemble a dragon was, in reality, the first complete imprint of an Ichthyosaurus. Even today, you can still find traces from ancient times as erosion constantly uncovers new fossils, especially after heavy storms.

The 500-metre-long pebble beach of Ladram Bay is bordered by towering, often bizarrely shaped cliffs (opposite).

LOCATION On the west coast of Finistère

SIZE 1,000km²

UNESCO Biosphere Reserve since 1988

Islands and Sea of Iroise
FRANCE

The Biosphere Reserve of the Islands and Sea of Iroise includes the islands of Ouessant, Molène and Sein, as well as the surrounding Sea of Iroise. The origin of the name Mer d'Iroise is disputed among linguists, but a theory popular among the local population seems too plausible not to be believed. According to this theory, the name comes from the Old French word "ire", meaning wrath. And anyone who visits can see for themselves that the Sea of Iroise is indeed a wild one, raging with fury. At times, the waves of the Atlantic lash against the western end of Brittany with such force that it seems as though they might smash the rocks to pieces. While this creates a spectacular sight for visitors on land, for sailors, it is a passage that commands the utmost respect. This is why the coastline is dotted with small, picturesque lighthouses, which warn ships of the dangerous currents.

The small island of Ouessant, covering only 15 square kilometres, lies at the westernmost point of France and marks the beginning of the English Channel.

LOCATION On the triple border of France, Italy and Switzerland: in the French department of Haute-Savoie, the Italian region of Aosta Valley and the Swiss canton of Valais

SIZE 645km²

Mont Blanc Massif
FRANCE

No other mountain in Europe commands more respect or evokes more fear than Mont Blanc, the highest peak in the Alps. First mapped in 1606, it was given the ominous name Montagne Maudite, the cursed mountain. It was believed that ghosts, demons and other devilish creatures inhabited the summit. No one dared to climb it. Even when the Genevan naturalist Horace-Bénédict de Saussure offered a reward in 1760 for the first person to reach the summit, it wasn't until 8th August 1786 that Jacques Balmat and Gabriel Paccard stood on top of it. The following year, Saussure himself conquered the mountain. His famous quote upon reaching the summit became part of Mont Blanc's history: "The soul soars, the mind seems to expand and amidst this majestic silence, we believe we hear the voice of nature".

The summit of the Aiguille du Midi (3,842 metres), affords the most stunning view of Mont Blanc (4,809 metres), the highest peak in the Alps.

LOCATION Region of Provence-Alpes-Côte d'Azur, departments of Alpes-de-Haute-Provence and Var
SIZE 1,930km^2
ESTABLISHED 1997
parcduverdon.fr

Verdon Regional Natural Park
FRANCE

In June, the landscape around the town of Valensole transforms into a unique, fragrant sea of blossoms. The lavender, which is cultivated on vast fields here, blooms in full splendour before the harvest begins in August. Its intense fragrance and vibrant colour attract not only numerous tourists but also bees and bumblebees, which cannot resist this temptation and bestow upon the region with a local speciality, lavender honey. The Bee Museum in Valensole honours the important work of these industrious creatures, which, in addition to pollinating the lavender fields, also pollinate the region's almond trees. The northern part of the Plateau de Valensole, located in the midst of the Verdon Regional Nature Park with its gigantic gorge, is unusually forested and hilly, which is why it is not heavily cultivated.

Europe has its own Grand Canyon. It lies in Provence, is one of the largest natural wonders of France and is not overshadowed by its American counterpart, even though its dimensions are more modest: the Verdon Gorge is 21 kilometres long, up to 700 metres deep and, at its narrowest points, the rock walls are just six metres apart (left).

A violet sea of lavandin flowers, a natural hybrid of true lavender and spike lavender. It is cultivated for the extraction of essences and essential oils (above).

LOCATION Region of Provence-Alpes-Côte d'Azur, department of Bouches-du-Rhône, near Marseille

SIZE 520km²

ESTABLISHED 2012

calanques-parcnational.fr

Calanques National Park
FRANCE

Right next to the port city of Marseille lies the almost exotically beautiful Calanques National Park. The turquoise blue waters of the Mediterranean wash against high cliffs that are lushly covered with green plants. In addition to nearly 90 square kilometres of land, the nature park also includes around 430 square kilometres of marine area. The rugged limestone cliffs, which offer little space for soil but are situated right by the sea, create a unique flora and fauna. In addition to rare flowers and herbs, protected species such as corals, bats and even dolphins thrive here. For climbers and hiking enthusiasts, the park is a paradise, with various difficulty levels and ascents inviting visitors to spend a day in nature, enjoying the incredibly beautiful views over this verdant landscape and the Mediterranean.

The national park, just south of Marseille, proves that nature conservation and proximity to a city need not be mutually exclusive. The fjord-like coves of the Calanques with their limestone coastline are one of the largest tourist attractions in the south of France. It is an idyll where you can enjoy peace and recharge your batteries on a hike along the coast, for example.

LOCATION In the west of Schleswig-Holstein on the North Sea; the nearest town is Husum

SIZE 4,400km²

UNESCO World Heritage Site since 2009

nationalpark-wattenmeer.de/sh

Schleswig-Holstein Wadden Sea National Park
GERMANY

At times, this landscape radiates great tranquillity, while at other times it is relentlessly whipped by the raging elements. This seemingly endless expanse is an impressive sight, but just as striking is the wind and weather one experiences here. Germany's largest national park covers over 4,400 square kilometres, stretching from the mouth of the Elbe River to the Danish border. In the Middle Ages, much of this area was still solid land. However, frequent storm surges gradually eroded parts of it, leaving behind oddly shaped remnants: the North Frisian Islands, the Halligen and many small sandbanks. Twice daily, the sea releases its bounty and exposes a habitat that may initially appear inhospitable but is one of the most vibrant and sensitive ecosystems in existence.

The national park is home to numerous mudflat areas, as well as land areas almost completely covered with salt marshes and sand dunes. It hosts the largest number of birds in Europe, and one can also encounter grey seals and harbour seals sunbathing on the beaches (above).

LOCATION In the Elbe Sandstone Mountains, on the border with the Czech Republic

SIZE 93.5km^2

ESTABLISHED 1990

nationalpark-saechsische-schweiz.de

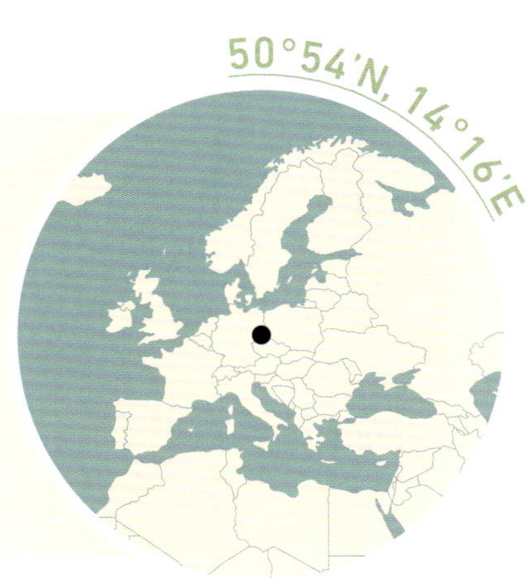

Saxon Switzerland National Park
GERMANY

Few landscapes captivated the Romantics of the nineteenth century as much as Saxon Switzerland: an idyllic river valley, lined with the equally picturesque and bizarre rock formations of the Elbe Sandstone Mountains. This landscape was shaped by erosion, which over millions of years has worn away the soft sandstone. The national park encompasses the most beautiful areas along the northern bank of the Elbe. One part stretches west of Bad Schandau, around the Bastei to Stadt Wehlen, while the other extends to the Czech border. These rugged rock regions were not only protected for their beauty, but also because the strong topographical division of the landscape has created a variety of different habitats where rare plant species can thrive.

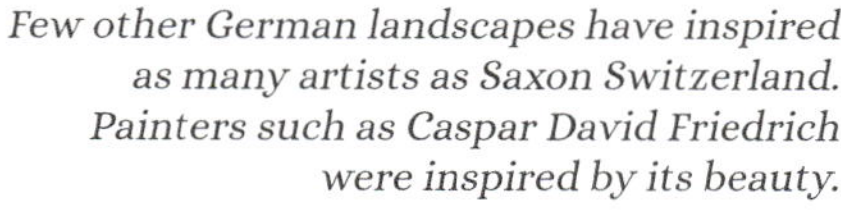

Few other German landscapes have inspired as many artists as Saxon Switzerland. Painters such as Caspar David Friedrich were inspired by its beauty.

LOCATION In the far southeast of Bavaria; between Ramsau, near Berchtesgaden, and Schönau on Königssee

SIZE 210km²

ESTABLISHED 1978

nationalpark-berchtesgaden.bayern.de

Berchtesgaden National Park
GERMANY

Germany's first and only high-altitude national park was founded in 1978, with the aim of creating a sanctuary for nature. The heart of Berchtesgaden National Park is the Königssee, surrounded by the Hagen Mountains, the Watzmann massif, the Hochkalter Mountains and the Reiter Alpe. Although the park is accessible by 230 kilometres of hiking trails, the entire area, apart from the tourist hotspots around the lake, is rather solitary. This allows for uninterrupted observation of majestic eagles, red deer, chamois, ibexes and marmots. The park is also home to insects, reptiles and amphibians. Rare plants, such as the lady's slipper orchid, edelweiss and dwarf primrose, can also be found here. Additionally, the park boasts many fascinating geological phenomena, such as the Funtensee, the Wimbachtal and the Blaueis Glacier.

Watzmann

The Watzmann massif is undeniably the king of the Berchtesgaden Alps. With a height of 2713 metres, its distinctive shape towers over the Berchtesgaden Land. Crossing the three main summits – Hocheck, Mittelspitze and Südspitze – is considered one of the most challenging hikes in the Bavarian Alps: a total of 2,100 metres of altitude must be overcome and several sections require climbing skills. The east face, at 1,800 metres, is the highest continuous rock face in the Eastern Alps and is both a dream and a nightmare for many mountaineers. The massif is also home to a diverse flora and fauna, with rare alpine plants such as the wild alpine violet, which no longer occur in the Bavarian Alps, thriving here.

The two highlights of the national park, the Königssee and the Watzmann massif, are located right next to each other.
The majestic Königssee: it is only possible to walk from Schönau to St. Bartholomä about once every ten years. The last time the Königssee froze over was in 2006 – for a total of 29 days.

LOCATION On the Swiss–Italian border, in the canton of Valais, and the Italian regions of Piedmont and Aosta Valley

HEIGHT 4,478 metres

Matterhorn
SWITZERLAND

What hasn't already been written about this mountain? The Matterhorn has been showered with superlatives, its incomparable shape praised; it has even been called the "Peak of Advertising" because its image has been used on everything from Swiss yoghurt pots and Belgian beer bottles to wine labels. It has adorned a cigarette box from Jamaica and even a Rolling Stones tour poster (1976). A mountain as a myth, and yet much more than just a rock pyramid. The Matterhorn owes its iconic shape to glacial erosion, with two layers of rock lying at an angle to one other. Since the beginnings of European mountaineering in the nineteenth century, climbing this mountain has been regarded as the ultimate challenge. The first successful ascent was made by the Briton Edward Whymper in 1865.

At 4,478 metres, the Matterhorn is one of the giants of the Alps. The mountain is Switzerland's landmark: no matter which angle you photograph it from, it always shows its best side.

The reflection of the Matterhorn on the Stellisee is truly an impressive natural spectacle, especially when the sun catches the upper third of the pyramid, making it glow brightly (right).

LOCATION In the federal states of Salzburg, Tyrol (East Tyrol) and Carinthia; large areas on both sides of the main Alpine ridge, around Großvenediger and Großglockner, extending down into the valleys

SIZE 1,856km^2

ESTABLISHED 1981 (Carinthia)

hohetauern.at

High Tauern National Park
AUSTRIA

Spanning over 1,800 square kilometres, the High Tauern are the last large natural landscape in the Eastern Alps, located between the Wildgerlostal in the west and the Lungau Murwinkel in the east. It was declared a national park in 1981, mainly due to its unique flora and fauna. Austria's highest peaks, more than 30 mountains over 3,000 metres, are found in the "core zone". These glacier-capped ice giants, with their jagged peaks, form a line stretching towards the horizon. And between the steep rock faces, crystal-clear glacier streams rush down the valleys. The "outer zone" has been shaped by human activity: a near-natural composition of blooming alpine meadows, lush mountain pastures and dark protective forests. The villages in the main valleys form the "cultural zone". The locals have long embraced sustainable tourism, while education and research also play a major role in the national park.

The mountain landscape around the Großglockner (opposite and left) offers numerous hiking trails and is home to the alpine marmot (above). The view of the glaciers from the Kaiser-Franz-Josefs-Höhe viewpoint is spectacular (main picture).

LOCATION Southeast Poland, near the city of Zakopane
SIZE 210km²
ESTABLISHED 1954
tpn.gov.pl/tatra-national-park

Tatra National Park
POLAND

The High Tatras protect a multitude of treasures: 27 species of orchids, including the extremely rare yellow lady's slipper; dozens of animals and plants that are found nowhere else in the world, such as the Carpathian monkshood and the Tatra scurvy-grass; 650 caves; waterfalls up to 70 metres high; and a mysterious lake called Morskie Oko, which is believed to have an underground connection to the ocean. The mountain range stretches between Poland and Slovakia, and includes Poland's highest peak, the 2,499-metre-high Rysy. It's a world full of wonders and legends, watched over by sleeping giants of stone, who could awaken at any moment to defend their well-guarded idyll and the chamois, marmots, brown bears, lynxes, wolves and otters found here.

Sunrise in the Tatras: steep mountain slopes await climbers (main picture), while the more gentle slopes of the Giewont massif are easily hiked (opposite bottom).

A blanket of fog hides the towering walls of the High Tatras, which emerge in full view as the day progresses, while lake eyes and waterfalls add variety to the landscape (right and opposite top).

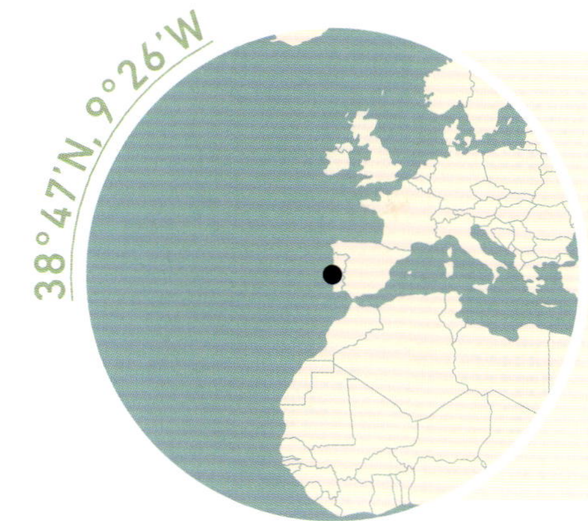

LOCATION Lisbon District
SIZE 145.83km²
ESTABLISHED 1994
UNESCO World Heritage Site since 1995

Sintra-Cascais Natural Park
PORTUGAL

Nature doesn't get much more diverse than in the Sintra-Cascais Natural Park: cliffs dropping into the sea, solitary lakes, half-ruined houses and villages, untouched sand dunes and centuries-old architecture. Among its attractions are the area's geological wonders and the waves of the Atlantic. The area, covering 145 square kilometres, stretches from the hills of Sintra to the beaches of Cascais. It has long since been granted World Heritage status. More than 200 species of vertebrates, nine different freshwater fish, over 170 bird species, 20 reptiles and 34 mammal species have been found in this region, west of Lisbon. The natural park offers countless opportunities for hiking and sightseeing – more than can be accomplished in a single holiday.

Praia da Ursa

The beaches around Sintra are as varied visually as the coastline itself. Gently sloping sandy beaches alternate with pebbly coves, some sheltered between rocks, while others are exposed to the raging Atlantic. No matter the time of day, the rock needles of Praia da Ursa always cast a special spell – whether in the morning when the sun reaches only their tips, or later in the day from the hiking trails above the cove and its turquoise water. It is most magical at dusk, when the sun has set and the sky takes on ever-changing hues. With its crescent-shaped sandy beach, the bay can only be reached on foot, so visitors sometimes encounter guided hiking groups here.

Access to Praia da Ursa is not entirely easy, but those who manage are rewarded with a beautiful part of nature. The beach is considered one of the most stunning in the region.

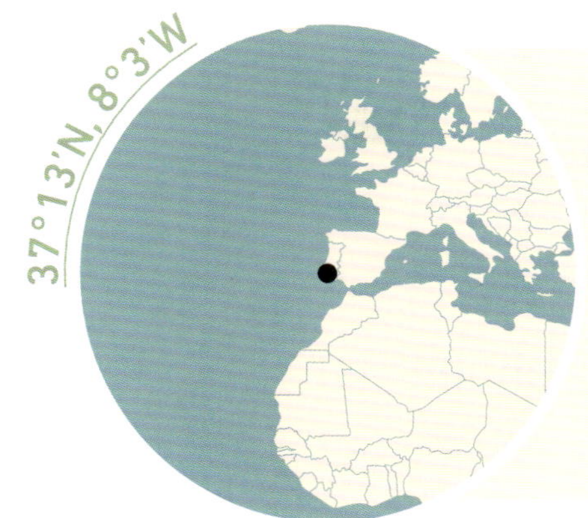

LOCATION The Algarve stretches from the southwesternmost point along the Atlantic coast to the Rio Guadiana at the Spanish border, covering three sections: Costa Vicentina, Barlavento and Sotavento

SIZE 4,989km²

Algarve Coast
PORTUGAL

The Algarve is the southernmost of Portugal's historical provinces and encompasses the same area as the Faro District. Its special charm comes from a variety of landscapes: rugged sandstone cliffs open up to hidden coves in the west; wide, cliff-lined sandy beaches define the central Algarve; and to the east, land and sea seem to merge into islands, channels and sandbars. Enchanting cities like Tavira and Lagos have preserved their picturesque old towns and laid-back atmosphere.

Each of the Algarve's 100-plus beaches has its own character, including Praia da Dona Ana (above left). The sandstone cliff landscape known as "Piety Point" (Ponta da Piedade) is also a must-see (left).

LOCATION Northern coast, between Santander and Cuchía
SIZE 17.53km²

Costa Quebrada
SPAIN

Between Santander and Cuchía stretches the so-called "broken" coast. Indeed, its rugged and bizarre rock formations give the impression that a powerful fist has shattered the landscape into pieces. Among the most famous rocks are the stone columns of Urros de Liencres, which stand like lost guardians protecting the coast. The 20-kilometre Quebrada Coast is designated a UNESCO Global Geopark due to its unique geological features. Those who embark on one of the guided tours offered in the park will learn how tropical reefs and vast forests once shaped this landscape. Particularly fascinating is the nocturnal tidal walk, which offers an insight into the marine fauna at the foot of the cliffs.

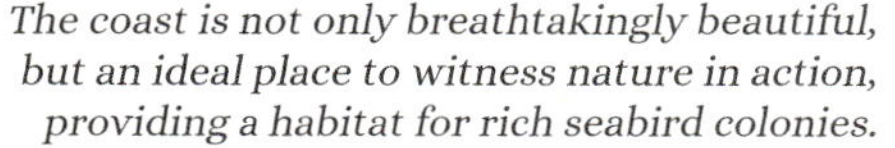

The coast is not only breathtakingly beautiful, but an ideal place to witness nature in action, providing a habitat for rich seabird colonies.

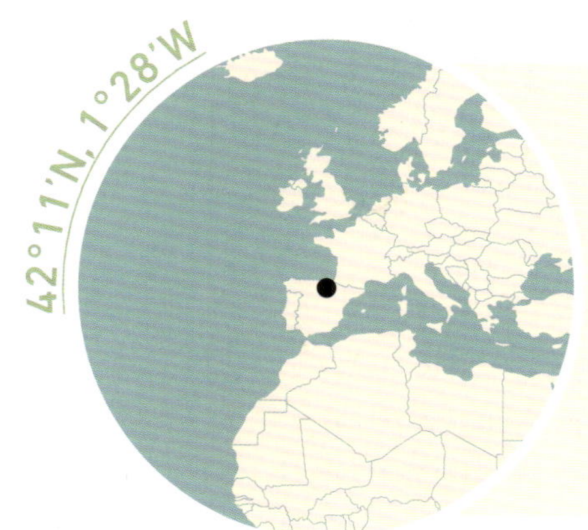

LOCATION Navarra Province
SIZE 393km^2
UNESCO Biosphere Reserve since 2000

Bardenas Reales
SPAIN

In the fifteenth century, Spain had several kings, both legitimate monarchs such as the Kings of Castile and self-proclaimed ones like the cruel Sanchicorrota, who declared himself King of the Bardenas Reales. With his band of thieves, he terrorized monasteries, villages and cities in this inhospitable region in the south of Navarra. In 1452, the real king, Juan II of Aragon, had had enough. He cornered the bandit but could not capture him, as the villain took his own life with a knife. Today, the Bardenas Reales is one of Spain's most breathtaking landscapes: a mosaic of constantly changing topographies, at times resembling a lunar landscape of ravines and craters, at others a desert of magnificent ochre, then a steppe or savannah. In 2016, filming for the series *Game of Thrones* took place here.

The wind current Cierzo is responsible for the erosion that has shaped these unique rugged landscapes, canyons and plateaus. Extreme temperatures prevail here, with only the most resilient creatures surviving.

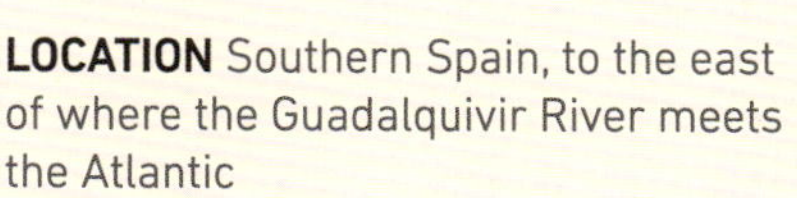

LOCATION Southern Spain, to the east of where the Guadalquivir River meets the Atlantic

SIZE 542km^2

ESTABLISHED 1969

UNESCO World Heritage Site since 1994

Doñana National Park
SPAIN

The defining characteristic of the Doñana National Park is its varied landscape. In addition to vast marshlands with lagoons and swamps, there are dry areas with heath- and savannah-like vegetation. In the dry zones, sand dunes as high as 40 metres give way to Mediterranean shrubland, where rare plant species such as white thyme grow. There are also forests of cork oak and umbrella pine. The wetlands serve as nesting grounds for numerous bird species, including a large population of flamingos, while grey herons, storks and cranes also nest within the park. Depending on the season, countless different bird species can be observed in this vast natural paradise. Migratory birds perform a remarkable feat of navigation and energy management. Their most important "major airport" in Western Europe and one of the world's most significant breeding sites is located here in the Guadalquivir river delta.

Bright colours as a warning or more subtle patterns for camouflage: the Iberian lynx (main picture), bee-eater, hoopoe, purple swamphen, lapwing, bluethroat and spoonbill (clockwise from above left), as well as the ocellated lizard (above), all have fundamentally different survival strategies.

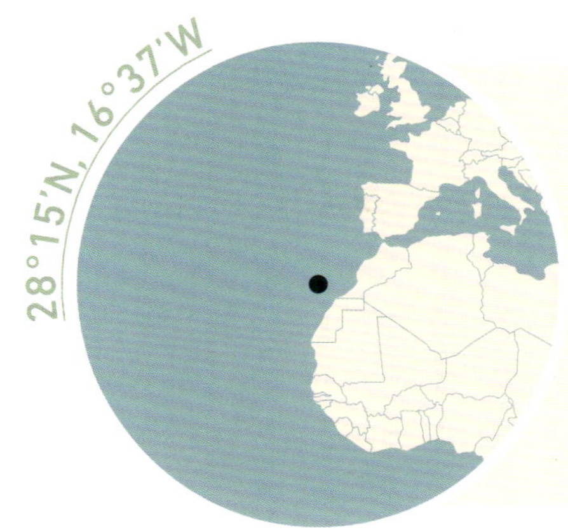

LOCATION Tenerife, Canary Islands
SIZE 190km²
ESTABLISHED 1954
UNESCO World Heritage Site since 2007

Teide National Park
SPAIN

The landscape of Teide National Park on the island of Tenerife is a fascinating result of millions of years of volcanic activity. The park covers an area with a diametre of approximately 17 kilometres and an average altitude of around 2,000 metres. In some places, the terrain resembles a barren, moon-like landscape; nevertheless, a remarkable flora has developed, having adapted to the extreme conditions. One of the most notable plants is the viper's bugloss, a perennial that can grow up to three metres high. Among the park's most outstanding geological formations are the rock pinnacles of Los Roques, which rise about 30 metres into the sky. A hiking trail leads visitors through fascinating lava formations, whose colours range from deep black and brown to shades of blue-green.

The entire national park is a geological treasure, offering a unique variety of volcanic phenomena and breathtaking landscapes. This stunning scenery has not only gained recognition for its natural beauty but has also repeatedly served as a backdrop for film productions.

LOCATION At the northeastern edge of the Dolomites, on the border of the Italian provinces of South Tyrol and Belluno

UNESCO World Heritage Site since 2009

hochpustertal.net

Sexten Dolomites
ITALY

The Sexten Dolomites form the northeasternmost mountain range of the Dolomites. They lie in the far east of South Tyrol and in the northern part of the Belluno province. To the north, they are bordered by the Puster Valley, to the east by the Sexten Valley, to the south by the Val d'Ansiei and to the west by the Höhlenstein Valley. The Three Peaks Nature Park, located in the South Tyrolean part of the range, has been part of the Dolomites UNESCO World Heritage Site since 2009. The Sexten Dolomites are primarily composed of dolomite rocks that formed from coral reefs in a primeval sea. The contrast between gently rolling meadows and the towering reef peaks rising up from them is characteristic of the area. Some of these peaks exceed 3,000 metres in height, typically surrounded by massive debris fields. The nature park is home to significant populations of grouse, including snow grouse, rock grouse, willow grouse and capercaillie.

The Cristallo massif, as seen from the Dürrensee. It is thought that the rock layers of the mountain were built up over millions of years in a warm primeval ocean on a slowly sinking coral reef (above).

Passo di Giau is considered one of the most beautiful and popular passes in the Dolomites – not only does the Giro d'Italia pass through it, but also the Dolomites Marathon, and it is frequented daily by countless cyclists and motorcyclists (right).

LOCATION South of Aosta, at the border between the Aosta Valley and Piedmont
SIZE 710km²
ESTABLISHED 1922
www.pngp.it/de

Gran Paradiso National Park
ITALY

The Gran Paradiso National Park, located in the Graian Alps, was the first national park to be established in Italy, granting it the highest level of protection. The park stretches from 800 metres up to the highest peak, Gran Paradiso (4,061 metres). It offers mountaineers the opportunity to tackle their first 4,000-metre peak, as its ascent is considered relatively easy. At the top, the scenery truly lives up to the park's name, making you feel like you're in paradise. A popular hike is to the Nivolet plateau (2,500 metres), which is home to several lakes. With luck, you might encounter an Alpine ibex – the symbol of the national park. The Italian royal family decided to protect the area as early as 1821, imposing a hunting ban that was extended to include themselves in 1913. In recent years, wolves and griffon vultures have returned to the area, further adding to the park's wilderness allure.

While hiking, it's common to encounter animals such as ibex, marmots, chamois, hares, weasels, stoats and foxes. Foxes can live as high as 2,500 metres and prey on young ibex. This is true wilderness.

LOCATION Central Italy, in the regions of Umbria and Marche; the visitor centre is located in Montefortino

SIZE 697.2km²

ESTABLISHED 1993

sibillini.net

Monti Sibillini National Park
ITALY

Sometimes nature rolls out a red carpet and every hiker gets to feel like a head of state. In the Monti Sibillini in Umbria, nature seems to be expecting a dozen leaders, showering her meadows with poppies in abundance. This sweet and delicate picture could have been taken from a child's drawing. However, the Monti Sibillini are far less harmless than they seem. Demons are said to live here and – seemingly mocking the bright red – they practice dark magic. But the most dangerous is the prophetess Sibyl, who dwells deep in the mountain, surrendering herself to all earthly sins. Sometimes she leaves her grotto to lure lost wanderers with her sibylline chants – to their doom or, perhaps, to the peaks, as the landscape is at its most beautiful beyond the treeline.

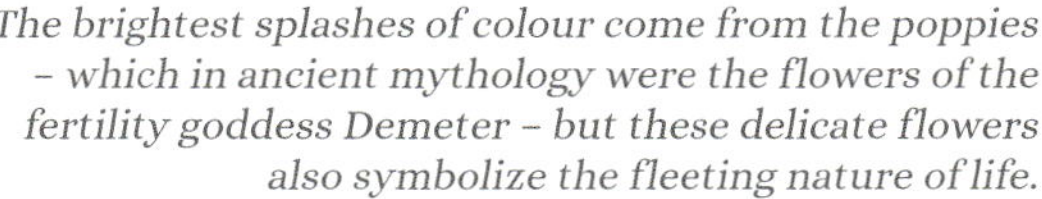

The brightest splashes of colour come from the poppies – which in ancient mythology were the flowers of the fertility goddess Demeter – but these delicate flowers also symbolize the fleeting nature of life.

LOCATION Northwest Italy, along the coast of the Liguria region

SIZE 38.6km^2

ESTABLISHED 1999

UNESCO World Heritage Site since 1997

Cinque Terre National Park
ITALY

The park is part of the Cinque Terre cultural landscape, which is a UNESCO World Heritage Site. The "Five Lands" form a twelve-kilometre stretch of coastline dotted with five villages: Monterosso, Vernazza, Corniglia, Manarola and Riomaggiore, with a total of around 5,000 residents. All five villages are surrounded by towering cliffs, some several hundred metres high, which drop dramatically into the turquoise-blue sea. Colourful houses, are spectacularly located either directly on the water or perched on cliffs and many of the slopes are terraced for grape and olive cultivation. The ancient mule tracks that pass through the national park are some of Italy's most popular hiking routes. However, the region's breathtaking beauty comes with a challenge: the area sees a influx of 2.5 million visitors each year. In order to address this, an entrance fee for the trails was introduced in 2002.

Strict regulations protect this stunning coast – cars have been banned, buses run on gas, and coastal fishing and underwater hunting have been restricted since the park was established. Offshore, a Marine Protected Area in the Mediterranean Sea between Liguria, Tuscany, Sardinia, Monaco and the French Riviera, protects cetaceans, such as the striped dolphin.

LOCATION Southern Limestone Alps, in the Slovenian regions of Upper and Inner Carniola, and the Italian region of Friuli Venezia Giulia

SIZE 1,957.23km^2

UNESCO Biosphere Reserve since 2003

Julian Alps
SLOVENIA

The Julian Alps are named after the Roman Emperor Gaius Julius Caesar, as both were deemed to share a sense of greatness. Many centuries later, UNESCO has acknowledged this by designating the region from northwest Slovenia to northeast Italy as a Biosphere Reserve, offering it special protection. The highest mountain in the Julian Alps is Mount Triglav, at 2,864 metres, which has been under the protection of a national park since 1981. The biosphere concept aims to balance human activity with nature conservation and this is reflected in the region, where agriculture, including farming, dairy, forestry, fishing, water management and cheese production, provide income. However, tourism is becoming increasingly important.

The crystal-clear waters of the Sava River shine against the stunning backdrop of the Julian Alps. The largest river in Slovenia originates at the foot of Mount Triglav.

LOCATION Located in the karst region of central Croatia, near the border with Bosnia and Herzegovina

SIZE 269.85km^2

ESTABLISHED 1949

UNESCO World Heritage Site since 1979

np-plitvicka-jezera.hr/de

Plitvice Lakes National Park
CROATIA

The Plitvice Lakes National Park, which spans approximately eight kilometres, owes its formation to limestone deposits and land subsidence over thousands of years. These natural processes have created barriers and dams made of calcified tufa, behind which the water has accumulated. The presence of algae and mosses gives the 16 large lakes their mesmerizing blue and green hues. The most impressive waterfalls, some of which drop as far as 76 metres, are found in the area of the four lower lakes. At the end of these lakes, the Plitvica River flows into the Korana River. Declared a national park in 1949, the area is situated at the foot of the Mala Kapela mountain range and is rich in flora and fauna. The dense forests are home to about 120 species of birds, along with deer, wolves and brown bears. In the 1960s, the region became famous as the filming location for several Karl May novels, including *The Treasure of Silver Lake* and *Winnetou*.

The fragile travertine barriers separate the breathtakingly beautiful cascades of the lakes. These natural stone water staircases pour the water in a never-ending flow, creating 16 waterfalls within the park. The largest waterfall, Veliki Slap ("The Great Waterfall"), forms where the Plitvice River plunges into the depths.

43°9'N, 19°2'E

LOCATION Northern Montenegro, surrounded by the Durmitor massif
SIZE 390km^2
ESTABLISHED 1952
UNESCO World Heritage Site since 1980

Durmitor National Park
MONTENEGRO

If you want to understand why the Balkans have a history of exhausting, endless wars without victors, you will find an answer in the mountains of northern Montenegro where combatants can survive for years whilst continuing the fight. The Durmitor, with its wild jumble of peaks, gorges and plateaus, once served as an impregnable fortress for resistance fighters. The landscape here is so overwhelming that it swallows people whole like ants – if you don't learn humility in the face of nature here, you won't anywhere! The 80-kilometre-long Tara Gorge is the second deepest gorge in the world, after the Grand Canyon, at 1,300 metres. Furthermore, there are 48 peaks above 2,000 metres, the highest being Bobotov Kuk.

Rocky mountains, rubble and water carving its own path through nature: the Durmitor National Park is like a raw diamond of nature. The Tara Gorge (right) is a haven for all kinds of outdoor activities

The park provides a pristine habitat for wild wolves (above right) and brown bears (above) who pose a real threat to livestock, such as sheep and horses.

LOCATION The Bucegi Mountains, part of the Southern Carpathians
SIZE 326.63km^2
ESTABLISHED 1974

Bucegi Natural Park
ROMANIA

In Bucegi Natural Park, in the Southern Carpathians, there is an aged version of the Great Sphinx of Giza. The rock formation is also called the Sphinx, but unlike its Egyptian counterpart, it is of natural origin and features a deep hole that resembles an eye. This monolith, along with the mushroom-shaped Babele Stones, are among the unique features of this natural park in Romania. Tourists visit for hiking or skiing and often stay at the surrounding huts. The well-developed reserve offers plenty of variety for both adults and children, with its 34 caves and waterfalls. The most popular are the Ialomitei Cave and the Ratei Cave, as well as other bizarre rock formations.

Transylvania is surrounded by numerous legends and eerie tales. However, nature often tells very different stories: of bizarre rock formations and gentle mountain valleys – as seen here in the Bucegi Natural Park.

Not as intricately detailed as its Egyptian counterpart, but carved by Mother Nature: the Sphinx of Bucegi (above).

LOCATION The Pirin Mountains, Blagoevgrad Province, southwest Bulgaria

SIZE 403.32km^2

ESTABLISHED 1963

UNESCO World Heritage Site since 1983

Pirin National Park
BULGARIA

Bulgaria faces a challenge as a travel destination, often being reduced to the Black Sea Coast and, at best, its Byzantine monasteries. Less well known is the fact that Bulgaria is a true Garden of Eden, despite the Pirin National Park in the southwest of the country being designated a UNESCO World Heritage Site in 1983. The park was recognized for its "extraordinary beauty" due to its alpine landscape, with 70 glacial lakes, countless waterfalls, striking peaks and idyllic alpine meadows – features that could easily make one forget the Black Sea beaches. For mountain lovers, this remains a hidden gem. It is one of Europe's most beautiful wildernesses.

The Pirin National Park was named after Perun, the highest god in Slavic mythology. And indeed, the nature here, in all its splendour, feels truly divine. Ancient black pines grow in the forests, chamois roam freely (above), and falcons and eagles soar in the skies. The conditions in the Pirin National Park truly seem paradisiacal.

LOCATION In the eastern Pindus Mountains, in Thessaly
SIZE 272km^2
UNESCO World Heritage Site since 1988

Metéora
GREECE

North of the town of Kalambaka lies one of the great sights of Greece – a rock formation known as the Metéora. Visitors are greeted with a breathtaking view, as the valley is home to a series of towering rock pinnacles on which 24 monasteries were built over time. Only a few of them are still inhabited today. The Megálou Meteórou is the highest, founded around 1360 by Saint Athanasios, the Bishop of Alexandria. On another high rock stands the Monastery of Nikoláou Anapavsá, founded around 1388. The Varlaám Monastery, built in 1517, was named after the hermit who erected a church in the same location in the fourteenth century. It is accessible via a bridge and was converted into a museum between 1961 and 1963, to display valuable monastic treasures. The Monastery of Roussánou is recently inhabited again by nuns.

The name Metéora means "suspended in the air", which aptly describes the location of these monasteries. The towering sandstone pinnacles of the Metéora are nearly inaccessible, rising several hundred metres into the sky.

LOCATION The island of Zakynthos, in the Bay of Laganas

SIZE 135km²

ESTABLISHED 1999

nmp-zak.org/ent

Zakynthos National Marine Park
GREECE

Zakynthos, the third-largest of the Ionian Islands, is located at the southernmost tip of the archipelago. It is known for its stunning white-sand beaches and towering cliffs that drop into the crystal-clear waters of the Ionian Sea. These picturesque beaches are ideal for relaxing in the sun, but also play a crucial role in the conservation of the loggerhead sea turtle. The Kalamaki Beach, stretching over five kilometres, is one of the Mediterranean's most important nesting sites for this protected species. Thanks to an environmental initiative, a National Marine Park was established in 1999, following significant efforts to protect the area. Today, special metal frames secure turtle nests buried in the sand and sections of the beach are closed off to protect the hatchlings. In addition, motorized vehicles are restricted in certain areas.

The turtles lay their eggs on the beach and, after depositing them, the females immediately return to the sea, leaving them unattended.

Another famous spot on the island is Navagio (Shipwreck) Beach, located in the northwest near Anafonitria, which can only be reached by boat.

AFRICA

LOCATION Surrounding Toubkal, in the centre of Morocco
SIZE 380km²
Establishment of Toubkal National Park: 1942

High Atlas
MOROCCO

Rising to 4,000 metres, the "roof of Morocco" stretches from the Atlantic coast towards the Algerian border. In some places, its ridges drop steeply to the sea or vast plains, and in others the peaks of the High Atlas merge into gentle hill chains. Snow remains in the higher altitudes until late spring, making it possible to ski in certain areas. The High Atlas is also an important water reservoir for Morocco, feeding numerous rivers and lakes. Here lies the Toubkal National Park, centred around Mount Toubkal, which stands at 4,167 metres, making it the highest mountain in both Morocco and North Africa. Morocco's oldest national park was established in 1942 to preserve the unique vegetation and fauna of the High Atlas for future generations. Characteristic plants include holm oaks and Aleppo pines. In the forests, one can find Barbary apes, Atlas squirrels, porcupines and striped hyenas; higher altitudes are home to Cuvier's gazelles and Barbary sheep, which are known for being agile and skilled climbers. The Berber people have made their home in settlements such as Oukaïmeden and Tinmal. In the past, they roamed the mountains with herds of goats as semi-nomads, but today, many work as mountain guides – the national park is a popular destination for hikers.

Waves of rugged terrain shape a ridge of the High Atlas between Ait Ben Ali and Bou Tharar, eventually leading to a plateau. While the mountain range stretches from the Atlantic Ocean in the west of Morocco almost to Algeria, only a few passes are navigable.

The Toubkal National Park is home to North Africa's highest peak and offers breathtaking hiking routes through stunning natural landscapes. Here, hikers may encounter North African spiny-tailed lizards and helmeted geckos (right top and bottom), desert horned vipers (centre) and Barbary apes (opposite).

LOCATION Ben Gardane, southeastern Tunisia
SIZE 63km²
ESTABLISHED 1991

Sidi Toui National Park
TUNISIA

Located just 20 kilometres from the Libyan border, the Sidi Toui National Park is entirely surrounded by the sands of the Sahara, characterized by steppes and dune areas. The park's rare flora and fauna must cope with extreme temperature fluctuations, ranging from around five degrees to well over 40 degrees Celsius. The only water source within the park is a gathering spot for various birds, including migratory species and resident birds such as the bustard, rock partridge and racing pigeon. In addition, the park is home to a number of protected mammals, such as oryx antelopes, golden jackals and fennec foxes. Reptile species like horned toads, chameleons, snakes, desert monitor lizards and wall geckos also inhabit the park.

Sidi Toui National Park hosts a diverse wildlife (from left to right): desert monitors, sand vipers and racing birds. It is also home to the fennec fox – the smallest of all wild dogs – with notably large ears that help with temperature regulation (above). Once extinct in the wild, the oryx antelope (main picture) is now a common sight in captivity, often found in zoos.

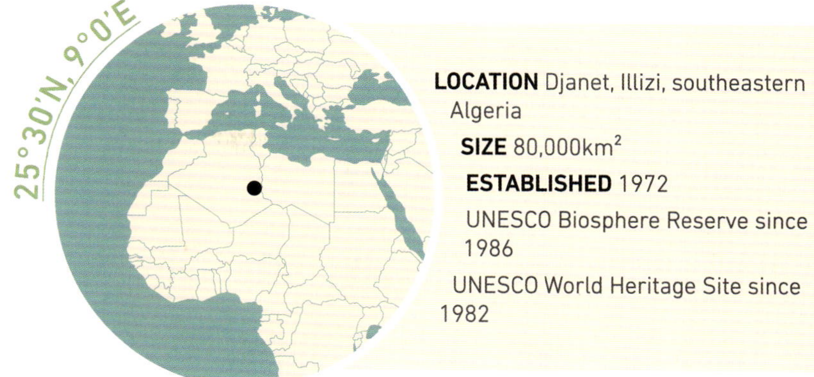

LOCATION Djanet, Illizi, southeastern Algeria

SIZE 80,000km^2

ESTABLISHED 1972

UNESCO Biosphere Reserve since 1986

UNESCO World Heritage Site since 1982

Tassili n'Ajjer National Park
ALGERIA

The ancient peoples who once inhabited the Tassili Desert in southeastern Algeria have left countless traces of their existence, primarily in the form of ceramics, but most notably through wall and cave paintings depicting animals and everyday life. Around 10,000 years ago, the region still had wildlife to hunt, fruits to gather and ample water for cultivating fields. However, gradually, drought overtook the desert, driving the people away. Other species managed to endure this transformation: the area is home to 28 native plant species, as well as mammals such as the dorcas gazelle and the Barbary sheep. Because of this, Tassili n'Ajjer is listed as a UNESCO World Heritage Site in recognition of both its cultural and natural significance, with the caves containing the rock art being surrounded by a vast national park.

The vast rock plateau of Tassili n'Ajjer, with its grotesque sandstone formations, dried-up riverbeds and deep gorges, resembles a lunar landscape.

LOCATION Ubari, Wadi al-Hayat, southwestern Libya
SIZE 58,000km²

Erg Ubari and Umm al-Maa
LIBYA

In the heart of the vast sand sea of the Erg Ubari in southwestern Libya, a chain of lakes serves as a reminder that the region was not always desert-like but once a fertile, moisture-rich area around 100,000 years ago. The remnants of this former abundance of water now present a nearly magical sight – the water surface of Umm al-Maa appears like a mirage amidst the red-golden dunes. Known as the "Mother of Water", this lake stretches several hundred metres in length, about 50 metres in width and reaches depths of up to ten metres. It remains a mystery as to why it hasn't silted up, despite sand continuously spilling from the surrounding dunes into the water, which has a high salt content. Around Umm al-Maa and the other Mandara Lakes, reed belts and palm trees provide a habitat for various animals.

For those who think deserts are just monotonous, the grand Erg Ubari in southwestern Libya proves otherwise. In this sea of sand, one can encounter not only animal inhabitants but even lakes.

A real Garden of Eden: when the dark blue Umm al-Maa appears with its green palms from the seemingly barren desert, it's almost unbelievable. At its shores, various species of agamid lizard can be found.

LOCATION Southern tip of the Egyptian Sinai Peninsula
SIZE 480km²
ESTABLISHED 1983

Ras Mohammed National Park
EGYPT

Covering approximately 480 square kilometres of land and marine areas, Ras Mohammed National Park is located at the southern tip of the Sinai Peninsula, a region that acts as the hinge between Asia and Africa, covering around 60,000 square kilometres. The park also includes the coastline of Sharm el-Sheikh: once an insignificant fishing village, this area has been transformed into a popular hub for beach and diving tourists. The underwater world here is mesmerizing, with even a short snorkelling session near the shore offering a delightful glimpse into its wonders. On land, however, the park appears sparse and barren, with only a few plants managing to survive in the sandy and gravelly dunes. Interestingly, the water-loving mangrove has deep roots in this harsh environment. Hundreds of bird species inhabit the park, making it a haven for birdwatchers.

Divers and snorkellers often find themselves awestruck by the beauty of the Red Sea, and anyone who has been surrounded by colourful damselfish can truly appreciate this experience (main picture).

Despite the vibrant beauty, caution is needed. Close encounters with poisonous creatures, such as the dwarf lionfish and the red lionfish, can quickly turn painful.

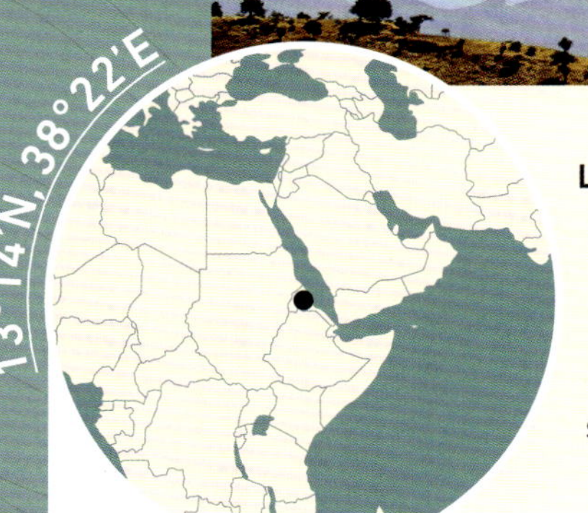

LOCATION Amhara Region
SIZE 412km²
ESTABLISHED 1966
UNESCO World Heritage Site since 1978
simienmountains.org

Simien Mountains National Park
ETHIOPIA

The Simien Massif, formed by volcanic activity 40 million years ago and later shaped by erosions, is now one of the most stunning landscapes in the world. With peak elevations around 4,500 metres, basalt gorges with raging rivers, jagged rocks and cliffs, and canyons as deep as 1,500 metres, the park's features create a breathtakingly dramatic image. Overlooking all of this is Ras Dashen, the highest peak in Ethiopia at 4,620 metres, which was first climbed by Europeans in 1841. The national park, named after the mountain range, provides a refuge for several rare species, including the gelada baboon, the Ethiopian wolf and the Walia ibex. In 1996, when the populations of the wolves and ibexes had fallen below critical levels, the park was included on the UNESCO List of World Heritage in Danger.

Spectacular is almost an understatement when describing the natural beauty of the Simien Mountains. Ras Dashen, the highest peak in Ethiopia, rises above 4,500 metres into a dramatically beautiful sky (main picture). The Walia ibex, Ethiopian wolf and gelada baboon (right images) inhabit the protected area.

LOCATION Southeastern Senegal, bordering the Senegal-Oriental and La Casamance districts along the Gambia River

SIZE 9,130km²

UNESCO World Heritage Site since 1981

Niokolo-Koba National Park

SENEGAL

A large part of the nearly 10,000-square-kilometre Niokolo-Koba National Park lies at the transition zone between the dry savannah and the humid Guinea forest zone. It is bordered to the south by the upper reaches of the Gambia River and Guinea's territory, while the northern part transitions into the eastern Senegalese dry savannah. The three major rivers of the Gambia system – the Gambia River, the Kouloutou in the west and the Niokolo-Koba in the northeast – drain the area in endless meanders with a gentle slope. Along the riverbanks, the tree savannah thickens into the lush vegetation of the gallery forests, home to around 200 species of trees and shrubs. The park is home to around 80 mammal species, including elephants, giraffes, chimpanzees and mongooses. It also supports one of Africa's largest lion populations, along with approximately 330 bird species, 35 reptile species, 20 amphibian species and 60 fish species, contributing to its rich biodiversity.

Due to a planned dam project and poaching, the park was added to the UNESCO List of World Heritage in Danger in 2007. It is one of West Africa's largest nature reserves and provides a refuge for savannah animals such as primates, antelopes, birds and bushbucks (above), whose habitat once extended to the coast.

11°53'N, 2°29'E

LOCATION West Africa, spanning northern Benin, southeastern Burkina Faso and southwestern Niger

SIZE 31,000km²

ESTABLISHED 1954

UNESCO World Heritage Site since 2017

W-Arly-Pendjari
NIGER · BURKINA FASO · BENIN

"W-Arly-Pendjari" refers to a unique cross-border complex of several protected areas that extend across the countries of Benin, Burkina Faso and Niger. Due to its diverse vegetation zones, which include grasslands, bush landscapes, wooded savannahs and gallery forests, this area provides a habitat for a wide range of animals, including those that are highly endangered or have disappeared from other parts of West Africa. Notably, it is home to the largest population of West African elephants and around 90 percent of all the remaining West African lions. Other large mammals, such as cheetahs, leopards, hippopotamuses and round-tailed manatees, also inhabit the W-Arly-Pendjari Complex.

The W-Arly-Pendjari Complex is home to several species of monkey, including chimpanzees, olive baboons and vervet monkeys. Like the endangered African savannah elephant (main picture), these species thrive in the wooded savannah. The Niger River (above), one of the primary sources of life for the area, flows through the entire complex.

LOCATION Northeastern Chad, in the Ennedi-Ouest and Ennedi-Est regions

SIZE 40,000km^2

UNESCO World Heritage Site since 2016

Ennedi Massif
CHAD

No other region in the Sahara embodies the term "lost world" as much as Ennedi-Tibesti, or as the nomads reverently and fearfully call it, "the land of hunger". The sandstone plateau of Ennedi is so isolated from the rest of the world that it is home to the most unusual creatures – for example, crocodiles that have become dwarf-sized due to millennia of isolation. There is no more than a handful of these creatures left, the last survivors of their kind, lingering at the waterhole like missteps of evolution. In ancient times, when the vast desert was still partly fertile land crisscrossed by rivers and marshes, armoured reptiles were abundant in the area. The last lions of the Sahara also live in Ennedi, but they will soon be as extinct as the sabre-toothed tiger, which used to tear into its prey with long canine teeth in this very region 12,000 years ago.

No waterhole in the Sahara is as well-known as the Guelta d'Archei in the northeastern part of Chad. It's not just typical desert dwellers who come here to quench their thirst, but also crocodiles. Guelta d'Archei is difficult to reach. If travelling from the capital N'Djamena, allow at least four days to get here.

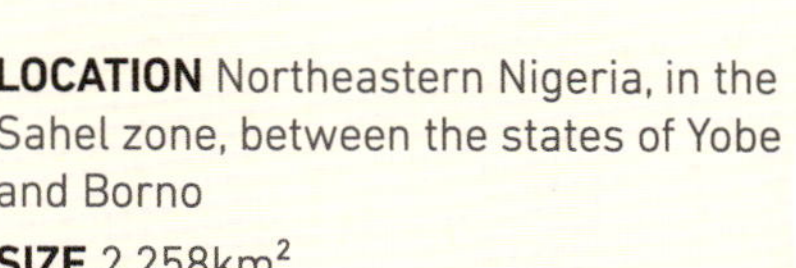

LOCATION Northeastern Nigeria, in the Sahel zone, between the states of Yobe and Borno
SIZE 2,258km^2
ESTABLISHED 1991

Chad Basin National Park
NIGERIA

The Chad Basin National Park spans a wide range of ecosystems, from arid and semi-arid to humid zones, covering areas from very dry to very wet. The park covers an area of 2,258 square kilometres and includes the Chingurmi-Duguma and Bulatura regions, as well as the Bade-Nguru Wetlands. The largest area, Chingurmi-Duguma, at 1,228 square kilometres, is a forest complex with dense stands of elephant grass. This area borders the Waza National Park in Cameroon. The Bulatura sector, with its captivating sand dunes and oasis-like, marshy valleys, resembles the desert and is unique to the landscape of Nigeria. The Bade-Nguru Wetlands around Lake Nguru are part of the Ramsar-protected Hadejia-Nguru-Bade area. The Dagona Birds Sanctuary within this region forms the centre of the national park.

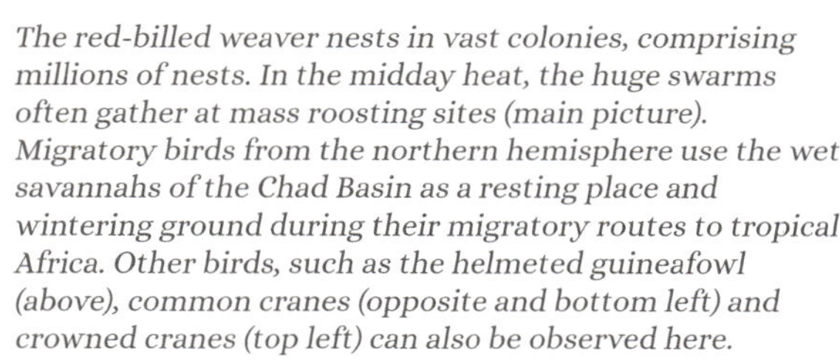

The red-billed weaver nests in vast colonies, comprising millions of nests. In the midday heat, the huge swarms often gather at mass roosting sites (main picture). Migratory birds from the northern hemisphere use the wet savannahs of the Chad Basin as a resting place and wintering ground during their migratory routes to tropical Africa. Other birds, such as the helmeted guineafowl (above), common cranes (opposite and bottom left) and crowned cranes (top left) can also be observed here.

LOCATION Far southwest of Cameroon, in the South Region; the area is mainly tropical rainforest and borders the Atlantic

SIZE 2,640km²

ESTABLISHED 1932

Campo-Ma'an National Park
CAMEROON

The Campo-Ma'an National Park is lush and green, characterized by both coastal and subalpine forests, up to an elevation of 800 metres. More than 1,500 plant species have been counted and ornithologists have recorded over 300 bird species. This protected area is rich in mammals and reptiles – crocodiles and sea turtles have been found in the Ntem River, and endangered forest elephants, chimpanzees, lowland gorillas and leopards also inhabit the park, while mandrills are recognizable by their distinctive red and blue faces. The park remains relatively underdeveloped for tourism, with only a few guides offering guided hikes or boat tours. Indigenous groups such as the Bagyeli Pygmies and the Bantu people live here, but are the park's protected status prohibits hunting or gathering in the area.

A river flows through the rainforest of the national park (right), which is the preferred habitat of the endangered mandrill (above).

LOCATION In the north, at the border with Sudan, where it forms a cross-border protected area together with the Radom National Park

SIZE 1,700km^2

ESTABLISHED 1960

André-Félix National Park
CENTRAL AFRICAN REPUBLIC

Mountain ranges and tree savannahs define this protected area on the border with Sudan. Established in 1960, shortly before the Central African Republic gained independence, it was the first national park in the country. Rivers such as the Lol, which is part of the Nile basin, originate from the Bongo Massif. The highest mountain reaches an elevation of 1,130 metres. Surrounding the park is a large buffer zone, the Yata-Ngaya Faunal Reserve, which is nearly four times the size of the national park itself. The fauna is dominated by typical savannah animals – giraffes, buffaloes, numerous antelope species and elephants roam the park, while lions and leopards hunt the herbivores. Hippopotamuses and crocodiles inhabit the rivers, and several hundred bird species call the park home.

Mammals in the national park include lions, warthogs and giraffes.

A large population of greater kudus lives on the park's border (main picture: a bull).

LOCATION In the east of the Democratic Republic of the Congo, at altitudes of 600 to 1,300 metres
SIZE 10,830km^2
ESTABLISHED 1970

0°30'S, 27°30'E

Maiko National Park
DEMOCRATIC REPUBLIC OF THE CONGO

This rainforest is one of the wettest regions in the Democratic Republic of the Congo. Situated at altitudes of up to 1,300 metres, it is classified as an afromontane forest, a special type of cloud forest. Due to its almost inaccessible location, it is home to many protected and endemic species. One of its most famous residents is the rare eastern lowland gorilla, but okapis and forest elephants also find a relatively undisturbed habitat here. The water civet, one of the rarest members of the civet family, is another endemic species. This remote park also provided a refuge for the Simba rebels for many years. Through resettlement and compensation programs, efforts are being made to give the rebels new homes in other areas.

Among the dense branches of the rainforest, it's possible to spot Senegal parrots (above), as well as okapis (opposite), eastern lowland gorillas (main picture) and crested mangabeys (centre and left).

LOCATION Uganda's Western Region, on the border with the Democratic Republic of the Congo

SIZE 996km^2

ESTABLISHED 1994

UNESCO World Heritage Site since 1994

0°13'N, 29°55'E

Rwenzori Mountains National Park
UGANDA

The mountain forests and marshlands of the Rwenzori Mountains provide habitat and protection for many endangered species, such as elephants, leopards and rock hyraxes. The highest peak of the range is Mount Stanley's Margherita Peak, at 5,109 metres. The mountain forests at higher elevations boast an extraordinary plant life. Lobelia, which usually grows to just 30 centimetres, can reach up to seven metres here. In sheltered spots, some ferns grow over ten metres tall and certain forms of heather are tree-sized. This giant growth is attributed to the combination of mineral-rich soils, stable temperatures, high humidity and the thick cloud cover that reduces the high ultraviolet radiation.

The Rwenzori Mountains often remain hidden beneath clouds, which is why they were discovered relatively late – many expedition groups simply passed by them. This mysterious and otherworldly landscape of lush green giants, transports visitors into another world. In this region, you'll find giant forest pigs, hornbills, tree hyraxes (clockwise from top) and diadem monkeys (above).

LOCATION Central Kenya, about 16.5 kilometres south of the Equator, roughly 150 kilometres northeast of Nairobi

SIZE 715km²

ESTABLISHED 1949, expanded in 2013

UNESCO World Heritage Site since 1978

Mount Kenya National Park
KENYA

When the devout missionary Johann Ludwig Krapf returned from an expedition deep into the heart of East Africa in 1849, he had an astonishing story to tell: in close proximity to the Equator, there was a mountain so incredibly high that its summit was perpetually covered with snow and ice. Despite Krapf swearing to the Almighty that what he had seen was true, no one believed him. Snow at the Equator? Glaciers in the tropics? What a bizarre notion! People concluded that Krapf must have been the victim of a hallucination and it wasn't until two years after his death in 1883 that a British expedition confirmed his account.

The second-highest peak in Africa, after Mount Kilimanjaro, Mount Kenya rises to 5,199 metres and is fully glaciated. Five distinct vegetation zones stretch from the plains to the summit, providing ample space for a unique array of plant and animal life.

1°29'S, 35°8'E

LOCATION Narok County, western Kenya; part of the Serengeti
SIZE 1,510km²
ESTABLISHED 1944
maasaimara.com

Maasai Mara National Reserve
KENYA

The Maasai Mara must be seen from above – either from an airplane or, even better, from a hot air balloon. The journey begins early, as only at dawn do the thermals of southern Kenya's grasslands allow for the flight. As the balloon silently ascends, the passengers fall silent, for what they see demands a quiet reverence: an endless wilderness, through which the Mara River snakes like a narrow brown ribbon. This is a world inhabited by tens of thousands, even hundreds of thousands, of wild animals: elephants, leopards, hyenas and wild dogs, wildebeest, gazelles and antelopes. Massive hippos, resembling living boulders, can be seen, as well as patiently waiting crocodiles, who may appear to be nothing more than logs. A lion pride rests nearby, and vultures and marabou storks circle overhead, the "garbage collectors" of the savannah.

One of the most spectacular scenes in the animal kingdom is the annual migration of the wildebeest in East Africa. During the rainy season, they graze on the lush pastures of the Serengeti in Tanzania. Once the rains cease in early summer, the land dries out and the wildebeest head north to the Maasai Mara in Kenya, where they must cross the Mara River. A torrent of bodies plunges into the water, hoping to reach the other side unharmed.

LOCATION Between Arusha in the southwest and the border with Kenya, the park encompasses several peaks of the Kilimanjaro massif

SIZE 1,688km²

ESTABLISHED 1973

UNESCO World Heritage Site since 1987

Kilimanjaro National Park
TANZANIA

Mount Kilimanjaro, standing at 5,895 metres, is part of the vast national park named after it. Like most of East Africa's mountains, Kilimanjaro is of volcanic origin. Rising 4,000 metres above the surrounding plains, it appears more majestic and unconquerable than many higher peaks in the Alps or Himalayas. Due to its position just south of the Equator, Mount Kilimanjaro displays a characteristic sequence of vegetation zones that mirror the horizontal transitions from the Equator to the polar caps. The savannah gives way to dense rainforest, which then transitions into a light mountain cloud forest. At around 3,000 metres, this forest gives way to a rocky, almost fairytale-like landscape where delicate lobelias grow. At 4,500 metres, the traces of ancient lava flows are clearly visible and, finally, one reaches the realm of eternal ice at the Kibo peak.

No matter from which perspective, Mount Kilimanjaro looks imposing, often surrounded by clouds that seem to emphasize its sheer size.

Viewed from the surrounding plains, the flat expanse at the summit is evident and, while the ascent is challenging, it remains relatively accessible.

LOCATION Northeastern Tanzania, on the border of the Serengeti National Park, north of Lake Eyasi and Lake Manyara

SIZE 8,094.4km^2

ESTABLISHED 1959

UNESCO World Heritage Site since 1979

Ngorongoro Conservation Area
TANZANIA

This conservation area covers the massive Ngorongoro Crater in northern Tanzania. Set against a dramatic landscape, it is home to thousands of wild animals, including gazelles, antelopes, waterbucks, zebras, elephants, hippos, rhinos, hyenas, lions and leopards. Humans and hominids have inhabited East Africa for around 3.6 million years and archaeological discoveries have led to the region being considered the "Cradle of Humanity". Stone and iron tools were found in the nearby Olduvai Gorge, as well as skeletons of *Homo sapiens*, *Paranthropus boisei*, *Homo habilis* and *Homo erectus*. In the Laetoli plain, fossilized footprints dated to 3.6 million years ago were discovered in 1978.

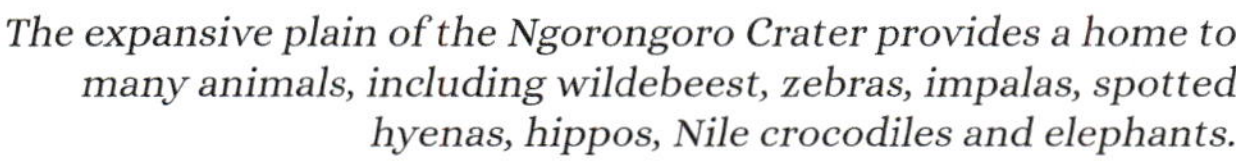

The expansive plain of the Ngorongoro Crater provides a home to many animals, including wildebeest, zebras, impalas, spotted hyenas, hippos, Nile crocodiles and elephants.

A view from the rim of the crater shows just how vast it is and, because few animals can climb the steep slopes of the crater to leave, it boasts the highest density of predators in Africa.

LOCATION Northern Tanzania, on the border with Kenya, extending across the regions of Mara, Shinyanga and Arusha, east of Lake Victoria

SIZE 14,763km^2

ESTABLISHED 1951

UNESCO World Heritage Site since 1981

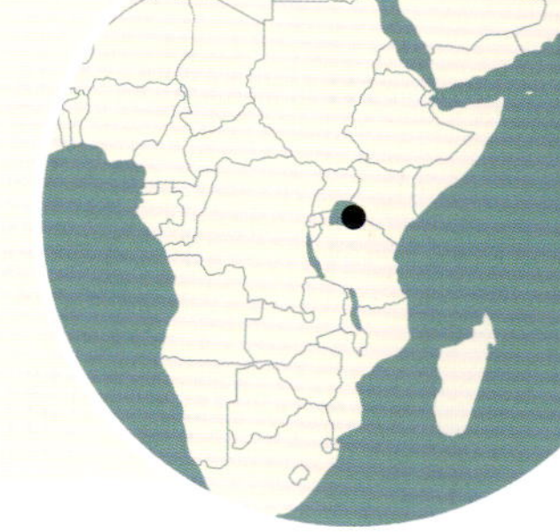

2°19'S, 34°50'E

Serengeti National Park
TANZANIA

The Serengeti is a vast savannah located east of Lake Victoria, stretching from northwestern Tanzania into neighbouring Kenya. Approximately 15,000 square kilometres of Tanzanian territory have been designated as a national park, which annually hosts one of the largest animal migrations in Africa. Enormous herds of more than two million Grant's zebras, wildebeest and Thomson's gazelles migrate in search of water and food through the steppe and savannah landscapes. Hot on their trail are their natural predators: lions, leopards, cheetahs and hyenas. In addition, giraffes, buffalo, topi and eland antelopes, hippos, rhinos, baboons, aardwolves, crocodiles, ostriches and elephants can be found here. A habitat with diverse fauna developed here over thousands of years, but this changed when Europeans invaded this wildlife paradise at the end of the nineteenth century and caused irreparable damage through big game hunting. The Serengeti was declared a protected area in 1921, and the Serengeti National Park was established in 1951.

In the Serengeti, no one is alone: the classic image of this landscape is shaped by large herds of animals, whether zebras or impalas. The wildebeest are the main players in the Great Migration. For about six months, they follow the life-sustaining rains through the Serengeti and into Kenya. The sunset behind the steppe grass and low trees has become an iconic symbol of this wild, untamed place.

LOCATION Angola, Namibia and the Western Cape of South Africa

SIZE 95,000km²

UNESCO World Heritage Site since 2013

Namib Desert

SOUTH AFRICA · ANGOLA · NAMIBIA

A UNESCO World Heritage Site since 2013, the Namib Desert is the world's only coastal desert where the dune fields derive their moisture from mist banks moving inland from the Atlantic Ocean. In good rain years, rivers from the Great Escarpment to the east can advance deep into the dune belts, creating small lakes, known as vleis, when the water evaporates. These salt-and-clay formations provide salt licks for wildlife. Sossusvlei and the surrounding dunes are some of Namibia's most fascinating natural attractions. The towering sand dunes, which can reach heights of up to 380 metres, cover ancient fossil dunes that were formed more than two million years ago. The reddish hue of the sand creates a breathtaking play of colours, especially at sunrise and sunset.

Nature effortlessly crafts the largest works of art, constantly changing as the wind, sun and desert interact, leaving behind footprints that never last. The landscape of the Namib is always in a state of flux, offering a dynamic experience for every observer.

LOCATION Northern Namibia, part of the Kalahari Basin

SIZE 22,935km²

ESTABLISHED 1907

Etosha National Park
NAMIBIA

Founded in 1907, Etosha National Park is named after the Etosha Pan, a vast salt pan located in the Kalahari Basin. The national park is home to over 2,500 elephants, who live in family groups led by matriarchs, with up to 50 calves, or in bachelor herds of up to eight bulls. These elephants should be approached with caution and their migration routes should not be obstructed. They typically visit waterholes during the night, but during the dry season, they may also seek refreshment in smaller family groups during the day. Elephants cool off by taking mud baths or spraying water over their bodies. Since they have no natural predators, they may monopolize the waterholes for hours, while other animals wait patiently for their turn. Early hunters who arrived in Etosha from South Africa in the mid-nineteenth century were amazed by the abundance of wildlife in this dry, salt-encrusted basin. For the Ovambo people, the area was an important source of salt for trading. The Haikom, a subgroup of the San people, once lived in the region as hunter-gatherers.

According to San legend, Etosha was the site of a terrible battle where only the women survived. Their tears, mourning the loss of their children, filled a lake and when the lake dried up, the salt pan remained. It is now a sanctuary for wildlife.

LOCATION Southern Zambia, bordering Zimbabwe
SIZE 66,000km²
ESTABLISHED 1989
UNESCO World Heritage Site since 1989

Mosi-oa-Tunya National Park
ZAMBIA

The first sign of the mighty Victoria Falls is visible from around 20 kilometres away in the form of a mist that rises up to 300 metres high. With a deafening roar, the Zambezi River, which forms the border between Zambia and Zimbabwe (making it a transboundary UNESCO World Heritage Site), plunges approximately 110 metres down. During the peak of the rainy season in March and April, the falls transform into a nearly two-kilometre-wide curtain of water, with up to 10,000 cubic metres of water crashing down per second. For the rest of the year, when the Zambezi carries less water, individual falls emerge, with the Rainbow Falls being the tallest among them.

The mist from the thundering water creates a magical atmosphere over the surrounding landscape, transporting visitors to an unexpectedly tropical world.

LOCATION Southern Malawi, near the eastern border with Mozambique
SIZE 2,400km²
UNESCO Biosphere Reserve since 2006

Lake Chilwa Wetland Biosphere Reserve
MALAWI

The dry and deciduous forests surrounding Lake Chilwa are among the oldest in Malawi. The lake itself consists of open water, marshes and floodplains, and the size of these areas fluctuates according to the season and related rainfall patterns. In the past century, the lake has completely dried out eight times. Typically, it fills up again, but in recent years, climate change has led to a gradual desiccation of the lake. The lake and wetlands, with their tropical climate, are an important habitat for birdlife. One hundred and sixty four different bird species have been recorded in the reserve, with some migratory species only inhabiting the area seasonally. Until the late nineteenth century, the lake extended to the base of the rugged granite peaks of Mount Mulanje. The impressive mountain massif is intersected by deep gorges and rivers that cascade down in waterfalls. Many of the region's more than 600 bird species breed in the steep cliffs.

The landscape is marked by expansive plains, interrupted by towering mountains. The Mulanje mountain massif formed through volcanic activity beneath the Earth's crust and its surface eroded, leaving behind tough granite rocks. Pelicans and the Northern Rock Python, which prefers marshland, are among the wildlife of the area.

LOCATION Southwest South Africa and the Kingdom of Lesotho
SIZE 2,493.13km²
UNESCO World Heritage Site since 2000

The Drakensberg
SOUTH AFRICA · LESOTHO

Stretching over 1,000 kilometres, the Drakensberg Mountains serve as a natural transition between South Africa's inland highlands and the eastern coastline. The northern part, known as the Transvaal Drakensbergs, is protected by the Blyde River Canyon Nature Reserve. The southern region, called the Natal Drakensbergs, features towering mountains over 3,000 metres high and secluded lakes, which have been part of the uKhahlamba Drakensberg Park since 2000, a UNESCO World Heritage Site. The park's largest treasure is the ancient rock art of the San people. Over 35,000 engravings and paintings have been discovered, much of it within the Giant's Castle Nature Reserve. More than 500 depictions of wildlife, hunting scenes and shamanistic rituals have been found at a single site alone.

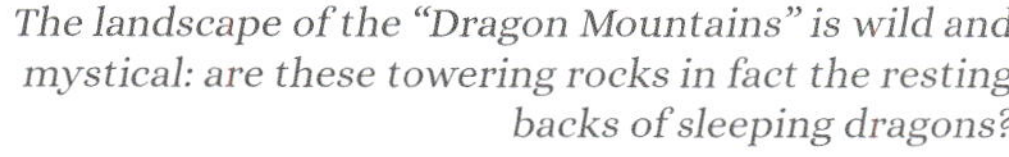

The landscape of the "Dragon Mountains" is wild and mystical: are these towering rocks in fact the resting backs of sleeping dragons?

One of the park's most spectacular features is the Tugela Falls, where the river plunges over the cliff edge and winds its way through the valley below.

LOCATION Eastern South Africa, within the northern Drakensberg, part of the Royal Natal National Park

HEIGHT 948 metres

Tugela Falls and Tugela Canyon
SOUTH AFRICA

In this region, hikers are treated to one of South Africa's most awe-inspiring natural spectacles. Tugela Falls (948 metres), the second-highest waterfall in the world after Venezuela's Angel Falls (979 metres), is fed by the Tugela River, which originates in the Mont-aux-Sources. On the journey to the falls, you pass notable landmarks including the Mont-aux-Sources (3,282 metres), Sentinel (2,165 metres) and Eastern Buttress (3,047 metres). For those seeking an adrenaline rush, there are two iron ladders fixed to the rocks, allowing you to climb 60 metres upwards. If the ladders feel too precarious, there is an alternative route through the Gully, a long, rocky terrain leading up to the plateau. Once at the top, a short hike brings you to the falls and the breathtaking view of the Drakensberg makes all the effort worthwhile.

LOCATION Western Cape Province, near Beaufort West
SIZE 768km²
sanparks.org/parks/karoo

Karoo National Park
SOUTH AFRICA

Established in 1979, the Karoo National Park, near Beaufort West, is dedicated to the protection of the unique flora of the Karoo region and the reintroduction of species that once roamed the area. The fragile balance of the Great Karoo was severely damaged by extensive sheep and goat farming, pushing it toward a barren desert landscape. In the national park, succulents and the characteristic Karoo bushes (known as "Bossies") now have the chance to recover from overgrazing. The park covers 80,000 hectares and features a variety of vegetation, typical of the lower plains and the Nuweveld Mountains, which rise to 1,911 metres. Animals commonly spotted here include kudu, oryx, springbok, plains and mountain zebra, wildebeest and eland antelope in the sparse, dry landscape.

The region is a semi-desert environment, with a name derived from the San language, meaning "dry".

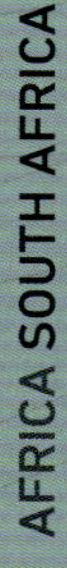

LOCATION Limpopo and Mpumalanga provinces, northeastern South Africa

SIZE 19,624km²

ESTABLISHED 1898

krugerpark.co.za

Kruger National Park
SOUTH AFRICA

The Kruger National Park, established in 1898, is one of Africa's largest and most renowned wildlife reserves. Covering nearly 20,000 square kilometres, it is South Africa's most popular tourist destination and a major source of foreign revenue. The park is crisscrossed with approximately 2,000 kilometres of roads, including both dirt paths and paved roads, providing access to the rich wildlife within. There are more than 20 "rest camps", offering accommodations ranging from basic campsites to luxury lodges.

The northern regions of the park are dominated by thornbush savannahs, while the vegetation becomes denser further south, where Mopane forests, grasslands and dense acacia groves provide homes for white and black rhinos, elephants, 17 species of antelope and a massive population of around 1,500 lions. Buffaloes wander the bush, giraffes browse from acacia trees and the park's incredibly diverse birdlife (over 500 species) adds to the symphony of sounds.

The Luvuvhu River runs through the Kruger National Park, providing a lifeline for many species, while lions and rhinos can be spotted in various areas, like the one shown here, resting and keeping a watchful eye on its surroundings.

LOCATION Northwestern Botswana; part of the Okavango Delta and one of the largest wetlands in Africa

SIZE 20,000km²

UNESCO World Heritage Site since 2014

okavangodelta.com

Okavango Delta
BOTSWANA

The Okavango Delta is one of the most extraordinary natural spectacles on Earth. During the rainy season, the Okavango River floods, creating a massive inland delta that can cover an area of 20,000 square kilometres within a few weeks. Streams become rivers, hills turn into islands and the land is transformed into water. This dramatic change is so intense that it is often likened to a modern-day flood, resulting in a vast wetland ecosystem that supports a wide variety of life. After six months, this watery world gradually recedes, returning the landscape to its previous form. This transformation attracts thousands of animals, creating a dynamic habitat for crocodiles, buffaloes, elephants, hyenas, wildebeests and hippos, among many other species.

The Okavango Delta is not just a marvel for its biodiversity but also for its ever-changing scenery, which is a spectacle to witness.

LOCATION In close proximity to the neighbouring islands of La Digue, Félicité and Sister Islands
SIZE 0.018km^2
ESTABLISHED 1996

Cocos Island Marine National Park

This Marine National Park consists of three small islands: Île Cocos, Île La Fouche and Île Plate, situated in shallow turquoise waters and surrounded by large coral reefs. Île Cocos, a miniature picturesque island, is only 18,000 square metres in size and located about one kilometre north of Félicité. Like the surrounding marine area, it has been under protection since 1996. This small granite island, with its picturesque palm vegetation, is a popular snorkelling destination and is often visited by boat from La Digue or Praslin. Above the large surrounding coral plateau, many reef fish such as rays, as well as moray eels, sea turtles and sometimes even whale sharks, can be found. For many years, boats were not allowed to anchor here to preserve the richness of the underwater world. It is therefore important, especially while diving and snorkelling, not to touch anything or to disturb the marine life.

LOCATION About six kilometres east of Praslin, 50 kilometres northeast of Mahé

SIZE 10km²

POPULATION 2,200

La Digue
SEYCHELLES

This 10-square-kilometre island can only be reached by boat. It is nicknamed "Île Rouge" on account of the reddish granite rocks that rise up to 300 metres in height in the bays around the island. In combination with the stunning white-sand beaches like Pointe Source d'Argent or Anse Source à Jean, the turquoise shimmering sea and the coconut palms that grow everywhere in between, the island presents a magnificent picture, often used as a backdrop for advertising or fashion shoots. There are no cars on La Digue. The island can be easily explored on foot, by bicycle or even by an ox-cart taxi. Inland, visitors can tour coconut or vanilla plantations and see how copra is processed into coconut oil. The Veuve Nature Reserve was created specifically for the paradise flycatcher, one of the rarest bird species in the world, which is found only on La Digue.

Grand Anse (main picture and above) on La Digue is a wild beach and its breathtaking setting makes it absolutely unique. However, it does not have a reef offshore and thus no protection from the open sea.

A miniature island and a popular excursion destination: Île Cocos (left) is the most popular snorkelling spot in the Seychelles.

LOCATION La Réunion, an overseas department of France in the Indian Ocean, 800 kilometres east of Madagascar

SIZE 2,512km^2

ESTABLISHED 2007

UNESCO World Heritage Site since 2010

Réunion National Park
LA RÉUNION

The first inhabitant of the secluded Cirque de Mafate crater on the island of La Réunion was an escaped Malagasy slave with a fearsome name: "Mafate", meaning "the Dangerous". Mafate ruled a community of escaped slaves for a large part of the eighteenth century before giving his name to the crater. The most difficult-to-reach of the three craters remains isolated: the 95-square-kilometre area of the northwestern caldera of Piton des Neiges can still only be visited on foot or by helicopter. Surrounded by mountains, including ten peaks over 2,000 metres, it forms a true protective wall. In addition, the area offers no less than 100 kilometres of hiking trails. Between forests, ravines and rocks lie small mountain villages, known as "Îlets", whose inhabitants happily welcome the numerous hikers. Since 2010, Cirque de Mafate, along with Cirque de Salazie and Cirque de Cilaos, has been a UNESCO World Heritage Site.

Cirque de Mafate is the driest and least known of the three craters, perhaps because it is only accessible on foot or by helicopter. As a result, it offers peace in pure nature.

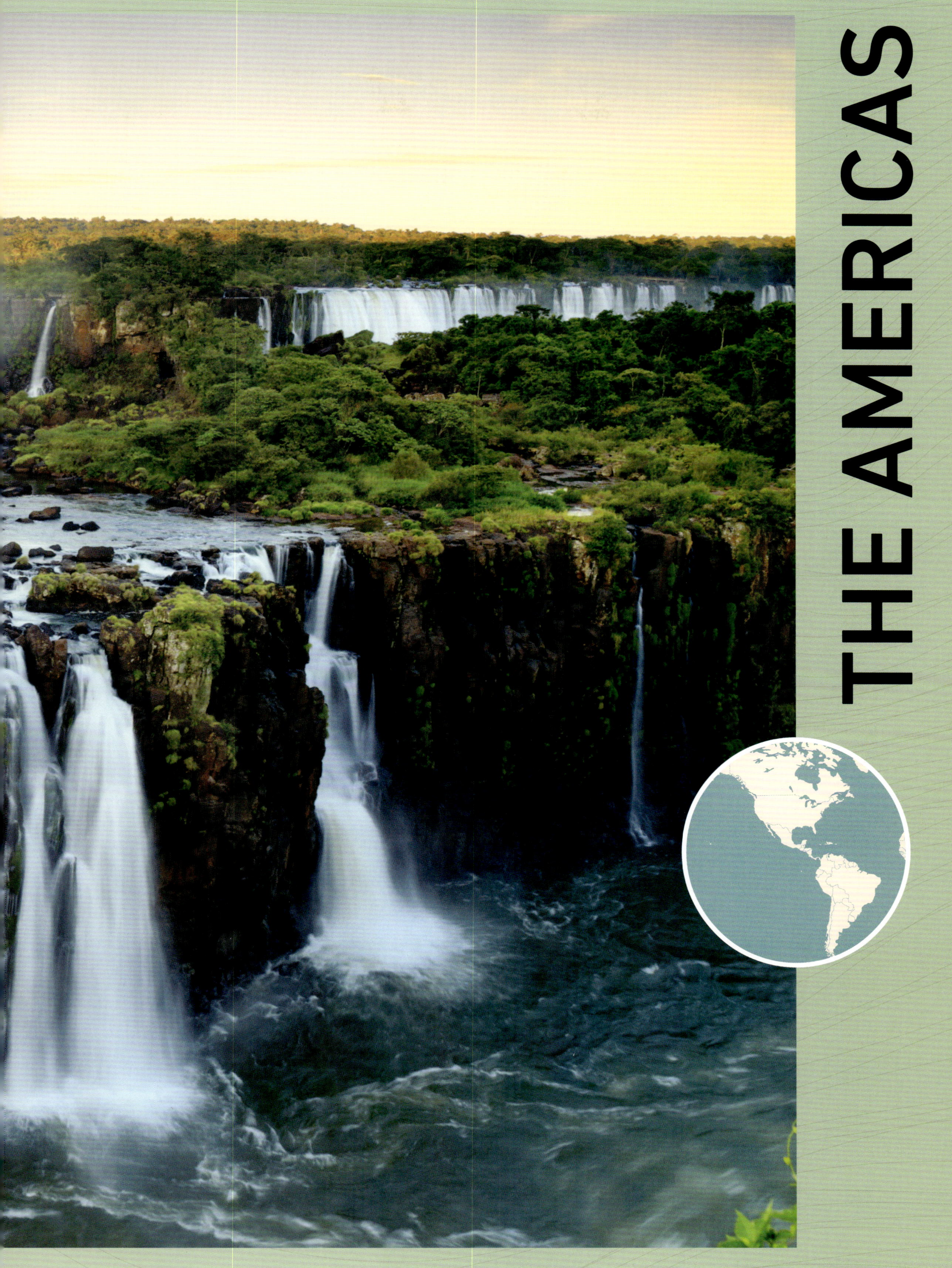

THE AMERICAS

LOCATION On the west coast of Vancouver Island off the coast of British Columbia

SIZE 511km²

ESTABLISHED 1970

parks.canada.ca/pn-np/bc/pacificrim

Pacific Rim National Park
CANADA

This national park borders directly the Pacific Ocean and stretches 130 kilometres along the west coast of Vancouver Island. Established in 1970, it became a reserve in 2001, with local indigenous peoples, primarily the Nuu-chah-nulth, participating in its management. The climate is cool and damp directly by the sea, and in this environment, lush rainforests have developed under towering Sitka spruces, ferns and moss. Large whales pass by in spring and autumn, marking a highlight for many travellers. Most visitors flock to the northern part of the park, at Long Beach near Tofino, where expansive sandy beaches and woodland trails invite leisurely walks. Further south, the Broken Group Islands appear scattered like pebbles. Hikers appreciate the 75-kilometre-long West Coast Trail, regarded as one of the best trekking routes in the world. Forest fires in 2024 caused a section of the park to be closed to visitors, in a startling reminder of the fragility of the environment it protects.

The national park is divided into three regions separated by water: Long Beach in the south of Clayoquot Sound; the Broken Islands Group, a collection of around 100 islands in Barkley Sound; and the West Coast Trail.

Bleached driftwood on South Beach: this is how the coast would have looked when Captain James Cook anchored here in 1778. To this day, the view stretches over an unspoiled landscape into the distance (opposite).

LOCATION In the Rocky Mountains, near the provincial capital of Edmonton in Alberta

SIZE 10,878km²

ESTABLISHED 1907

UNESCO World Heritage Site since 1984 (together with the Banff, Yoho and Kootenay national parks)

parks.canada.ca/pn-np/ab/jasper

Jasper National Park
CANADA

Canada as in the picture books: Jasper National Park in the Rocky Mountains is one of the most popular destinations in North America. Within its boundaries lie more than 800 lakes, most of which are fed by the surrounding glaciers. Beauvert Lake, a jade-green glacial lake, is located in close proximity to the town of Jasper. The Jasper Park Lodge situated on its shore became a successful competitor to the Banff Springs Hotel in the neighbouring Banff National Park. Jasper is less crowded than Banff, and on the trails in the hinterland, you can still experience the power of nature in peace. A mountain railway provides access to the much-visited Whistler Mountain for breathtaking panoramic views. Numerous trails lead into the remote, incomparably beautiful wilderness around Maligne Lake.

The water level of Medicine Lake (left), located at 1,436 metres above sea level and primarily fed by glaciers, fluctuates considerably. It reaches its highest levels in summer when the influx of meltwater exceeds the amount of outflow that can be drained through an underground river system.

From the Goat Lookout Point, one can gaze over the Athabasca Valley and get a sense of the vast expanse of the park: Jasper National Park is larger than its three neighbouring parks – Banff, Yoho and Kootenay (above).

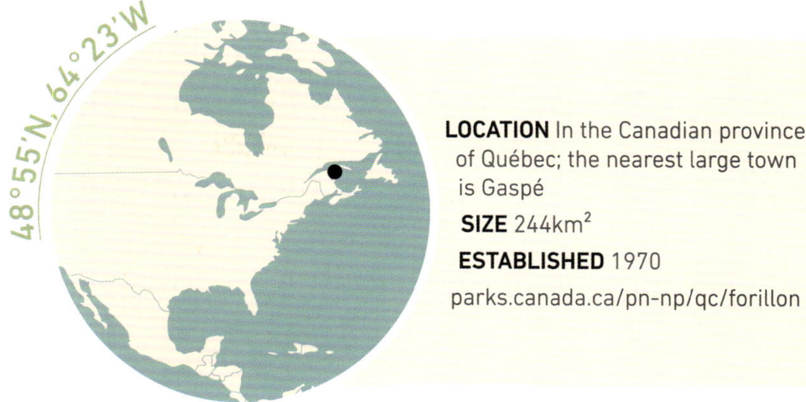

LOCATION In the Canadian province of Québec; the nearest large town is Gaspé

SIZE 244km²

ESTABLISHED 1970

parks.canada.ca/pn-np/qc/forillon

Forillon National Park
CANADA

Where the land ends: Forillon, established as Québec's first national park in 1970, lies on the long, narrow Gaspé Peninsula. Bordered by mountain ranges and sea cliffs, the St. Lawrence River flows into the gulf of the same name. Seabirds find a nesting paradise here, while Arctic plants meet alpine flora. Hiking routes lead from the dense forest, which gradually gives way to salt marshes, sand dunes and coastline. The best view of the 240-square-kilometre park is from the tower on Mont St. Alban, whilst at the tip of the rocky Cap Gaspé stands the tallest lighthouse in Canada. The Mi'kmaq and Iroquois once came to Forillon to hunt and fish. The Grande-Grave Museum Village vividly demonstrates how immigrant families made a living salting cod here in the nineteenth century.

The narrow, rocky Gaspé Peninsula juts far into the Gulf of St. Lawrence. From Cap Bon-Ami a dense forest in autumn colours can be seen, home to lynx, bear and porcupines (left).

Above: snowshoe hare and young northern harrier.

LOCATION In central Alaska, immediately west of the railway line connecting Fairbanks in the north to Anchorage in the south

SIZE 24,585km²

ESTABLISHED 1917

nps.gov/dena

Polychrome Pass

From here, you can enjoy a fascinating view of the surrounding mountains. Due to oxidized iron and other minerals, the rocks have intense colours, ranging from orange to rust red.

Denali National Park
USA

At the beginning of the twentieth century, thousands of fortune seekers flocked to what is now Denali National Park in search of gold. They dug through riverbeds, recklessly chopped down trees, left behind their rubbish and decimated the wildlife to feed themselves. There were no wildlife protection regulations at that time and conservation was unheard of. That is until the arrival of a naturalist called Charles Sheldon. Together with his companion Harry Karstens, he explored the land along the Kantishna River; they spent a winter in the mountains of the Outer Range and near the Toklat River. His passion for nature and tireless advocacy for the protection of this area led, after many years, to the founding of Denali National Park in 1917. Karstens, the first person to summit the mountain then known as Mount McKinley, became the park's first superintendent.

The taiga, the northern boreal forest, is the transition zone to the tundra. Here, the most beautiful autumn colours glow against the white peaks of the Alaska Range (right).

Caribou only fight during the rutting season when they have multiple cows in their harem and must defend their position (above). Otherwise, they are generally peaceful companions.

Toklat River

Charles Sheldon spent the winter of 1907–08 in a cabin by the Toklat River. He was so captivated by the landscape that he spent years fighting for the protection of the nature threatened by exploitation.

Wonder Lake

The lake, surrounded by willows and alders, stretches nearly six kilometres from north to south. If you're lucky, you might spot enormous moose wading in, feasting on the aquatic plants.

37°44'N, 119°35'W

LOCATION On the western slopes of the Sierra Nevada in California
SIZE 3,027km^2
ESTABLISHED 1890
UNESCO World Heritage Site since 1984
nps.gov/yose

Yosemite National Park
USA

Yosemite National Park is among the most impressive protected areas in the American West and is especially busy in the summer months. Yosemite Valley, located in the midst of one of the most forested areas of the Sierra Nevada, is particularly popular with visitors. The picturesque Merced River runs through the valley basin, while the granite cliffs surrounding it rise up to 1,500 metres. The idea of protecting Yosemite Valley was first proposed by Frederick Law Olmsted, the creator of New York's Central Park. However, it was the conservation pioneer John Muir who convinced the government to establish Yosemite National Park in 1890. His name is also synonymous with the protection of the giant sequoia.

Yosemite National Park is home to animals such as the lynx (above), mountain lion, black bear, white-tailed ptarmigan, American pika and coyote (right, from top).

Many visitors head to Yosemite Valley, where the famous Tunnel View overlook affords breathtaking views of the towering Cathedral Rock and El Capitan (opposite top). For about ten days in February, Horsetail Fall is bathed in the light of the setting sun, creating a fiery cascade (opposite bottom).

Devil's Golf Course

With such a rugged surface, only the devil could play golf, according to a description in a 1934 national park brochure. The valley was once the site of a pluvial lake, known as Lake Manly, whose water evaporated, leaving only a salt crust that has since been shaped into bizarre forms by the elements.

Mesquite Flat Sand Dunes

What would a desert be without dunes? Although these dunes are not even 100 metres high, they are among the most famous and easily accessible in the northern part of Death Valley. Their shapes vary from crescent-shaped to linear and star-shaped.

Artist's Palette

This is a literal colour palette. The slopes of the Black Mountains exhibit an incredible array of colours, caused by the oxidation of metals in the rock. Iron gives the red colour, copper results in green. The entire Artist Drive Formation is of volcanic origin.

LOCATION Eastern California, near the Nevada border

SIZE 13,628km^2

ESTABLISHED 1933 (National Monument); 1994 (National Park)

nps.gov/deva

Death Valley National Park
USA

Designated a National Park in 1994, the infamous Death Valley stretches across the far east of California, covering an area of around 13,000 square kilometres. It includes the desert valleys between the Panamint and Amargosa ranges, and temperatures in summer regularly exceed 50 degrees Celsius. The first white settlers who entered the valley nearly perished. Part of a wagon train heading for the California gold fields in 1849, they took what they thought was a shortcut and got stranded in the scorching heat. After surviving for 20 days, they were rescued and one of the settlers is said to have shouted, "Goodbye, Death Valley!", hence the name. Even today, traversing the valley requires extreme caution and sufficient water supplies are essential for survival.

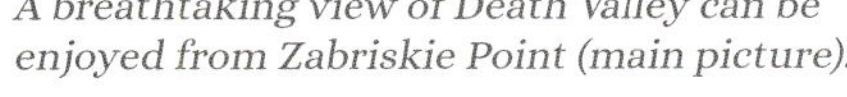

A breathtaking view of Death Valley can be enjoyed from Zabriskie Point (main picture).

Golden Canyon

The short hike through the "Golden Canyon" is one of the most beautiful you can take in Death Valley. The trail steadily climbs, leading through narrow passages and alongside towering rock walls. The canyon's rock shines in golden, reddish-brown and orange hues.

LOCATION Northwest Wyoming, in the Rocky Mountains, with sections extending into Montana and Idaho

SIZE 8,983.49km^2

ESTABLISHED 1872

UNESCO World Heritage Site since 1978

nps.gov/yell

Yellowstone National Park
USA

Founded in 1872, Yellowstone National Park is a majestic wilderness with mountains, rivers, lakes and over 300 geysers. Cold water sinks into deep heat chambers, where it is heated and then forced to the surface through narrow channels. The most reliable geyser, "Old Faithful", erupts approximately every 70 minutes, sending columns of boiling water soaring into the air. The Steamboat Geyser, which last erupted in 1978, is the world's highest geyser, with a fountain over 100 metres tall. Sulphur smoke hangs in thick clouds over the Norris Geyser Basin. Other highlights of the park include the Grand Canyon of the Yellowstone with its Upper Falls and Lower Falls, as well as the lesser-known Crystal Falls in between. The wildlife is surprisingly diverse: bison, bears and elk often venture close to the roads.

Geothermal activity creates true wonders in Yellowstone National Park. Microscopic organisms have adapted to the hot temperatures, giving the basins their unique colours.

Grand Canyon of the Yellowstone

The nearly 400-metre deep Grand Canyon of the Yellowstone in the west, with its waterfalls and large bison herds, offers a journey back in time to America before it was changed by European colonizers.

Upper Geyser Basin

With the highest concentration of geysers in the world, the Upper Geyser Basin is a major attraction, not least because it is home to "Old Faithful". However, the many other geysers and colourful mud pots should not be overlooked.

Lower Geyser Basin

Some visitors claim that the Lower Geyser Basin encapsulates all the features of Yellowstone in one spot – and they're not far wrong, at least when it comes to geothermal activity: geysers, hot springs, sinter terraces, fumaroles and mud pots all present themselves at their finest here.

Old Faithful

The reliability with which "Old Faithful" sends its water column into the sky has made it one of the most famous geysers in the world, which is reflected in the number of people who watch the spectacle every hour.

LOCATION Near the town of Moab, Utah, between Interstate 70 and the Arizona border
SIZE 1,365km^2
ESTABLISHED 1964
nps.gov/cany

Canyonlands National Park
USA

The Canyonlands in southeastern Utah are among the most exciting landscapes on Earth. The area, which was only accessible to Native Americans and experienced horse riders in the first half of the twentieth century, was declared a national park in 1964. Many hiking trails lead into the canyons and valleys, revealing a fairytale world of colourful rock formations. The Green and Colorado rivers wind through the rock formations like green ribbons. The Grandview Point Overlook offers a breathtaking view of the river's canyons, while trails from the Needles Visitor Center lead past the sandstone spires to the south. The remains of stone houses built by the Ancestral Puebloans are visible everywhere. Few visitors venture to the more remote Maze district, where nature is largely untouched.

Mesa Arch is as characteristic of Canyonlands National Park as the flat-topped mesas and the shades of red typically accentuated during sunrise and sunset.

Island in the Sky

A triangular area in the north, characterized by high dryness. Hiking trails here lead to spectacular panoramic viewpoints, such as The Neck, which offers a grand view of the rock formations and two winding rivers.

White Rim

A defining feature of the Island in the Sky region is the White Rim, a dazzling white rock layer that seems to stretch across the rocks, creating an interesting contrast with the red hues around it.

Dead Horse Point State Park

This state park lies directly next to Canyonlands National Park and is particularly impressive for its view of the Colorado River, which makes a dramatic 180-degree turn in the canyon. Several film scenes have been shot here.

The Needles

These beautifully striped rock formations stand proudly upright. They are especially beautiful in Chesler Park and a recommended hiking trail in the area is the Confluence Overlook Trail, which provides a good view of the confluence of the Colorado and Green rivers.

Angel Arch

It's hard to say it any other way – Angel Arch is extremely photogenic, even though it's not the only rock arch in Canyonlands National Park. It is named for its shape, which resembles an angel in profile, with a long cape, wings and a gently lowered head.

LOCATION Southern Utah, between the Grand Staircase-Escalante National Monument and Zion National Park; Bryce Canyon City, to the north, provides accommodation

SIZE 145km²

ESTABLISHED 1928

nps.gov/brca

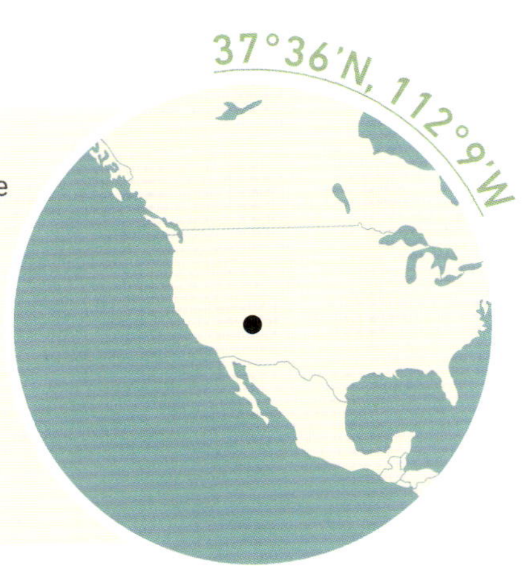

Bryce Canyon National Park
USA

The red rock towers of Bryce Canyon rise from the rocky ground like organ pipes. The colourful limestone formations, shaped by wind and weather over millions of years, have imaginative names like Thor's Hammer, Queen's Castle, Gulliver's Castle, Hindu Temples and Wall Street. Nowhere else, not even in the Grand Canyon, has nature been so capricious. John Wesley Powell was the first white man to explore the canyon around 1870. The park later got its name from Ebenezer Bryce, who built a ranch in Bryce Canyon but moved to Arizona as he often had to search for his cattle for weeks in the winding gorges. In 1924, this unique area, with its bizarre forest of sandstone spires, became a National Monument, and four years later, it became a National Park.

Anyone who visits Bryce Canyon will likely agree that nature sometimes creates the most beautiful and bizarre things. The edge of the Paunsaugunt Plateau extends over 30 kilometres, where wind and weather have carved countless rock spires – the Hoodoos. Here, even an annual one million visitors hardly make a noticeable impact.

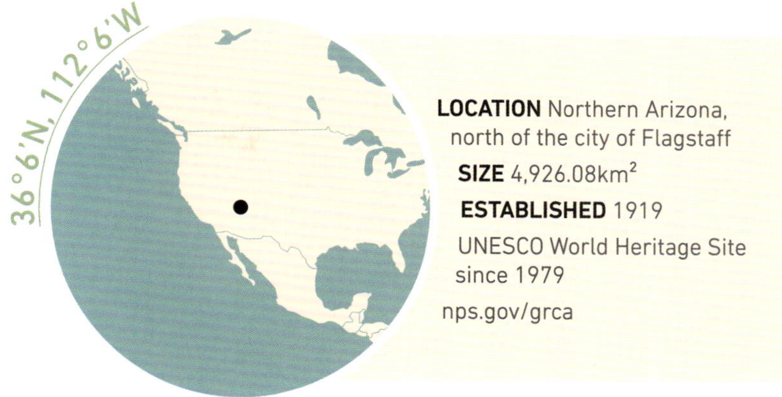

LOCATION Northern Arizona, north of the city of Flagstaff
SIZE 4,926.08km²
ESTABLISHED 1919
UNESCO World Heritage Site since 1979
nps.gov/grca

Grand Canyon National Park
USA

In 1540, the Spaniard López de Cárdenas was the first European to witness the grand panorama of the Grand Canyon, but it was not until the mid-nineteenth century that an accurate map of the area was created. The exact history of the Grand Canyon's formation is still not fully understood. It is believed that the river began carving its path through the plateau about six million years ago and, over time, a gorge formed. Wind and weather helped to create the canyon's unusually shaped walls, where clearly visible layers of rock document the various geological periods, and fossils found here provide important information about prehistoric life. The passionate conservationist John Muir once described it as "the greatest of God's earthly places".

The walls of the Grand Canyon drop almost vertically. To reach the other side of the canyon, one must travel around it, as the only bridges over the Colorado River are located outside the national park. Both canyon rims offer great viewpoints, especially during sunrise and sunset. Hiking tours allow for exploration of some of the side canyons, while helicopter tours offer a different perspective.

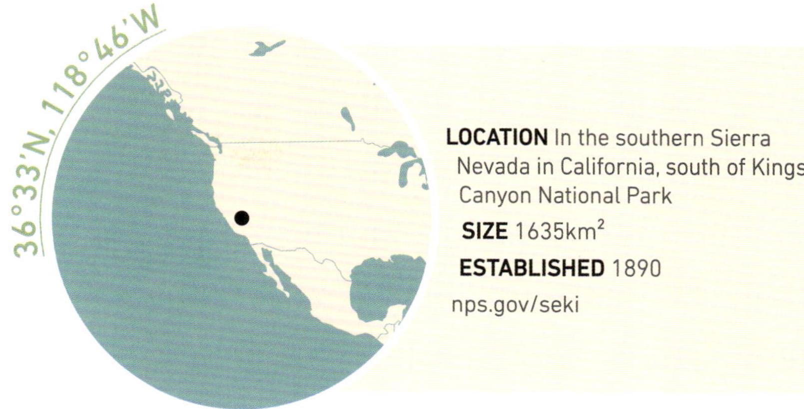

LOCATION In the southern Sierra Nevada in California, south of Kings Canyon National Park

SIZE 1635km^2

ESTABLISHED 1890

nps.gov/seki

Sequoia National Park
USA

Established in 1890, Sequoia National Park lies to the south of Kings Canyon. It is home to an entire forest of the giant sequoias which gave the park its name. Towering trees in all stages of growth can be found within the Giant Forest, and visitors can marvel at the largest living organism on Earth: the "General Sherman" tree, which measures nearly 1,500 cubic metres in volume. The ancient giant is estimated to be 2,000 years old, but could be as old as 4,000 years. Mountain lions, black bears, mule deer, coyotes and porcupines live in the forests and diverse hinterland of the 3,500-square-kilometre park. Birds of prey soar high, while songbirds – and eight species of bats – come much closer to visitors.

Sequoia National Park is famous for its population of giant sequoias: five of the ten tallest trees in the world grow in the Giant Forest. Visitors also make use of the park's hiking trails.

A cinnamon-coloured black bear (above) rests in the forest. In general, it is a skilled climber, a fast runner and a good swimmer.

LOCATION Southern Florida, near the city of Homestead

SIZE 6,104km^2

ESTABLISHED 1947

UNESCO World Heritage Site since 1979

nps.gov/ever

Everglades National Park
USA

The Everglades, a swamp area in the southern part of Florida, cover an area of 5,661 square kilometres. The national park, which was established in 1947, stretches from the Tamiami Trail in the north to Florida Bay in the south, and from the Florida Keys in the east to the Gulf of Mexico. The Seminole call the Everglades "Pay-hay-okee", meaning "sea of grass". When the wind blows over the Jamaica Sawgrass, the swamps resemble a stormy ocean. For centuries, the tough grass has been nourished by the water flowing south from Lake Okeechobee, but today the water is slowed down by artificial dikes and canals – an intervention in the natural cycle condemned by many ecologists. Boardwalks lead into the swamp areas, allowing visitors to observe the waterfowl while they are nesting. The seemingly impenetrable natural landscape of the Everglades is a paradise for wildlife. It is the only region on Earth where crocodiles and alligators coexist.

Like a turquoise sea, the salt marshes lie under a wide sky. Flora and fauna thrive in the brackish waters, in which freshwater from the north and seawater from the south dominate alternately.

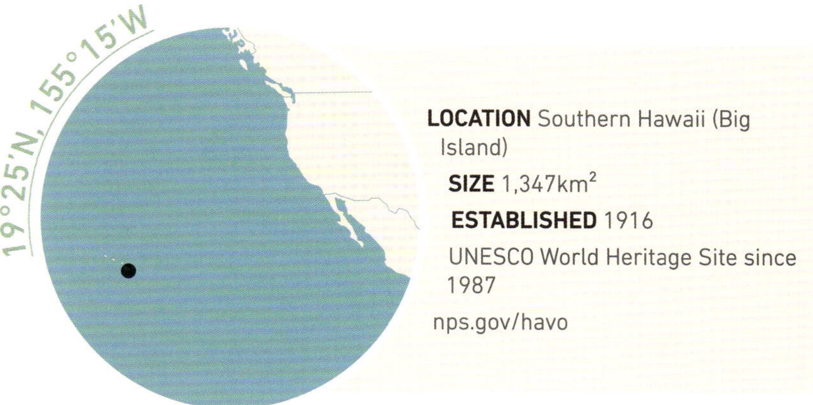

LOCATION Southern Hawaii (Big Island)

SIZE 1,347km²

ESTABLISHED 1916

UNESCO World Heritage Site since 1987

nps.gov/havo

Hawai'i Volcanoes National Park

USA

Established in 1916, this national park is located in the southern part of Hawaii's Big Island. It covers part of Mauna Loa, the still-active crater of Kilauea, as well as sections of the rugged coastline. The park spans a total area of 1,309 square kilometres. The 16-kilometre-long Crater Rim Drive loops around the Kilauea crater, while the Chain of Craters Road winds past numerous small craters and descends to the coast, ending at a safe distance from the flowing lava. Many viewpoints provide excellent insight into the lower volcanic craters. The strenuous Kilauea Iki Trail takes visitors six kilometres through tropical rainforest into a small crater and a 25-kilometre-long trail ascends to the summit of Mauna Loa.

Kilauea is currently one of the most active volcanoes on Earth. Its eruptions are effusive, meaning lava oozes from the earth's interior and flows in continuous streams.

LOCATION In the central eastern part of Quintana Roo state, on the Pacific coast northeast of the city of Felipe Carrillo Puerto

SIZE 5,280km²

UNESCO Biosphere Reserve since 1986

UNESCO World Heritage Site since 1987

Sian Ka'an Biosphere Reserve
MEXICO

Located 150 kilometres south of Cancún, this nature reserve provides an ideal habitat for over 100 species of mammal, numerous rare amphibians, around 350 different bird species and abundant tropical flora. The name of the reserve in the Mayan language means "gift of heaven". Indeed, the 5,000-square-kilometre protected area offers "heavenly" conditions for a unique fauna and flora. Mangrove swamps, mixed forests, rainforests, deciduous forests, palm savannahs, floodplains, coral reefs and lagoons provide a refuge for rare predators such as jaguars, various species of monkey, crocodiles and sea turtles. A quarter of the park area is water. In addition, Sian Ka'an contains 23 Maya archaeological sites.

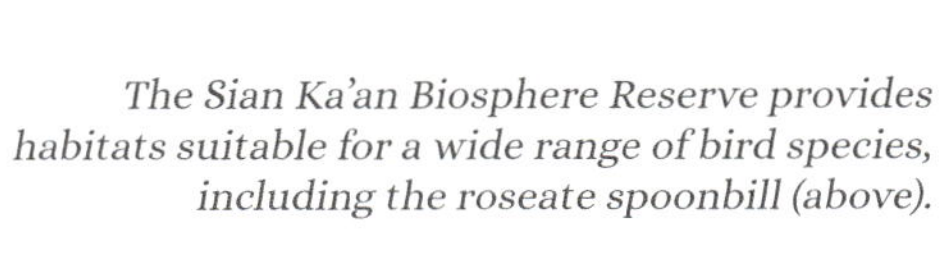

The Sian Ka'an Biosphere Reserve provides habitats suitable for a wide range of bird species, including the roseate spoonbill (above).

LOCATION In the south of Basse-Terre Island
SIZE 173km²
ESTABLISHED 1989
guadeloupe-parcnational.fr

Guadeloupe National Park
GUADELOUPE

"La Vieille Dame", as the cloud-covered Soufrière volcano is affectionately known, rises 1,467 metres into the Caribbean sky and is a defining feature of Basse-Terre, the westernmost island of Guadeloupe, an overseas department of France. La Soufrière is surrounded by nearly 17,000 hectares of dense mountainous rainforest, where over 3,000 different plant species have been recorded, including numerous orchid varieties. At the foot of "The Old Lady" lies the official capital of Guadeloupe: Basse-Terre. Its two baroque churches, dating from the 17th and 18th centuries, and the Fort Delgrès fortress make it a major attraction for visitors. To the northeast, lie cultivated fields amidst a gentle hilly landscape.

La Soufrière, located in Guadeloupe National Park, is the highest mountain in the Lesser Antilles (left). Above: the Carbet Waterfall (Les Chutes du Carbet).

LOCATION Along the river of the same name, from the eastern Caribbean coast to the interior of Honduras
SIZE 5,250km^2
ESTABLISHED 1969
UNESCO Biosphere Reserve since 1979
UNESCO World Heritage Site since 1982

15°44'N, 84°40'W

Río Plátano Biosphere Reserve HONDURAS

The biosphere reserve in the Río Plátano watershed encompasses a significant portion of the second-largest contiguous rainforest area in the world. Along the coast, behind pristine sandy beaches, there are lagoons and mangrove forests, as well as coastal savannahs with swamp plants, palms and lowland pines. Tropical and subtropical rainforests cover the interior, home to numerous tree species ranging from Spanish cedar to mahogany, balsa wood and sandalwood. Untouched by civilization, the reserve provides a pristine habitat for many animal species. Several thousand people live in this sparsely populated region, including the indigenous Miskito, Pech and Tawahka, as well as the Garifuna (an ethnic group with Caribbean and African ancestry), who continue their way of life here. The reserve is also an important archaeological site with remnants from the Maya civilization.

From the colourful to the dangerous: the fauna here ranges from toucans (main picture), scarlet macaws (centre) and white-shouldered capuchin monkeys to alligator lizards, boa constrictors, coffee snakes (left, from top) and ocelots (above). As well as Maya sites and wildlife, there are numerous plant species that bloom in magnificent colours and shapes which should not be overlooked (opposite).

LOCATION Located north of the capital San José. The biosphere reserve includes four national parks and other protected areas
SIZE 1,443.63km²
UNESCO Biosphere Reserve since 1988

Cordillera Volcánica Central Biosphere Reserve
COSTA RICA

Some areas of this mountain region appear remote and steep, as though never having been traversed by humans. Steep slopes are crisscrossed by a network of streams and rivers. Waterfalls cascade into the depths and lakes lie still like mirrors. The Cordillera Volcánica has many faces. Four national parks converge here, and there are two active volcanoes (Poás and Irazú), both of which are over 3,000 metres high. La Selva Biological Station plays an important role in preserving the tropical rainforest through its research on the 65 species of bats found here, along with many trees, lichens and plants, plus cataloguing over 5,000 species of butterfly. Rangers and volunteers are also working to curb poaching in the area, which primarily affects iguanas, deer and pacas.

A region of contrasts: barren volcanic rock and fire as the dominant element on one side, lush green vegetation and water on the other. And in between, the colourful great green macaws (right).

Poás

Volcanoes are among the most unpredictable natural phenomena on Earth. The 2,700-metre-high, still-active Poás is no exception and thus the park's opening times are also unpredictable. For nearly the entire year of 2017, visitors were not allowed near the volcano due to heightened volcanic activity in April – the government of Costa Rica deemed the risk too high. Although Poás has been relatively gentle over the past 100 years, only causing unrest in the 1950s, the last time residents of the nearby town Bajos del Toro had to be evacuated was in 1955. Nevertheless, the possibility of a larger eruption remains ever-present.

Irazú

If there is a place on Earth that comes closest to the Moon, it would probably be the crater area of the Irazú Volcano (3,432 metres). This comparison comes from a man who would know: Neil Armstrong. Those who reach the crater rim, on a clear day, not only see the two seas that surround Costa Rica but also the bright green lake in the belly of the fire mountain. It is an acid lake that changes colour depending on which gases are rising from below. The country's largest volcano is very active, having erupted as recently as 1994. Not only is its lava dangerous, but any changes in the crater are also perilous, as the wall surrounding the lake is thin. If the lake were to overflow, it would be a life-threatening catastrophe for the surrounding villages.

LOCATION In the Gran Sabana region of Bolívar state, southeastern Venezuela

SIZE 30,000km²

ESTABLISHED 1962

UNESCO World Heritage Site since 1994

Canaima National Park
VENEZUELA

In the language of the Kamarokoto Indians who live here, the name "Canaima" represents the dark deity that embodies all evil. In contrast to its frightening name, Venezuela's second-largest national park impresses with its overwhelming natural beauty. Located in the southeast of the country, at the border with Guyana and Brazil, the three-million-hectare park spans the epic landscape of the Gran Sabana. Nestled in dense vegetation, spectacular waterfalls such as Angel Falls, Kukenan Falls and the cascades of the Canaima Lagoon plunge into the depths. Between 3,000 and 5,000 species of flowering plants and ferns are said to be found here, many of them endemic. In addition to savannahs, there are also impenetrable mountain forests and scrubland. The diversity of orchids is impressive.

Angel Falls

When the American bush pilot Jimmie Angel spotted the waterfall from his airplane in 1933, he was captivated. He returned repeatedly to "his" waterfall and became its namesake. Initially, people at home thought his tales were "adventurer's talk" and did not believe that such a tall waterfall could exist. Today, Venezuelans also use the original name, "Kerepakupai Merú", which means "Jump of the Deepest Place" in the indigenous Pemón language. The name fits – after all, it was the local people who "discovered" the waterfall, not the foreign bush pilot. Still, this natural wonder is still known to foreigners as Angel Falls. Despite being located in a remote area, the waterfall has become one of the country's most popular tourist attractions. As back then, the region can only be reached by air – either by small plane or helicopter.

Angel Falls is the highest waterfall in the world: 978 metres deep, it plunges from the Auyán-Tepui plateau into the abyss (main picture).

On the high plateau, there is a unique microclimate. The weathered sandstone soil is nutrient-poor – the perfect ecological niche for many carnivorous plants like the pitcher plant (left).

LOCATION Approximately 60 percent of the Amazon Rainforest is within Brazilian territory, the rest is spread over eight other countries; it thus stretches over most of the northern half of the continent

LENGTH 6,992 kilometres

Amazon River and Amazon Rainforest
BRAZIL

Endless masses of water with countless islands covered in tropical rainforests: at the lower reaches of the Amazon, it is evident that it is far and away the most water-rich river on Earth. It carries more water than the next seven largest rivers combined! In wide meanders with numerous tributaries, it flows slowly and steadily through the largest contiguous rainforest area on Earth, a natural paradise that is home to 2,200 species of fish, 1,300 species of birds and 400 species of mammals, reptiles and amphibians. The Amazon is 4 to 10 kilometres wide at its lower course, after the confluence of the Rio Grande and the Rio Solimões. About 350 kilometres before it reaches the Atlantic Ocean, it splits into several main branches which open up into a funnel shape due to the high tidal waves.

The Amazon Rainforest is verdant, humid and almost impenetrable. It is one of Earth's most important green lungs and its mysterious darkness offers a habitat for rare species.

The Amazon is by far the most water-rich river on Earth: it discharges about 180,000 cubic metres per second into the Atlantic Ocean. It carries so much water that ships can travel from the river's mouth all the way to Manaus, about 1,500 kilometres inland, in the middle of Brazil.

LOCATION In the northeastern part of Goiás state, about 50 kilometres east of Lake Serra da Mesa
SIZE 6,480km²
ESTABLISHED 1961
UNESCO World Heritage Site since 2001

Chapada dos Veadeiros National Park
BRAZIL

The approximately 65,000-hectare national park extends through the northern part of Goiás state, in a mountainous area with average elevations of 1,400–1,500 metres, but reaching heights up to 1,800 metres. It forms a watershed, separating the tributaries of the Rio Maranhão and Rio Paraná. Founded in 1961, the park was later reduced in size and now covers only around one-tenth of its original protected area. The landscape is largely untouched, with only a few areas developed for visitors: for example, the two waterfalls of Rio Preto, with the first being about 80 metres high, spreading out in a fan shape into a vast bowl surrounded by steep cliffs. The second waterfall is even higher, reaching 120 metres.

The park covers the highest parts of the Cerrado region. Numerous rare species of animals are native here. A total of 45 mammal species, over 300 bird species and about 1,000 butterfly species have been documented.

Nature creates many forms of elegance: from the forked tail feathers of a tyrant flycatcher (right) and the velvety antlers of a pampas deer (centre), to the unique shapes of its flora.

LOCATION In the Brazilian state of Paraná, on the border with Argentina, where it continues as Iguazú National Park on the Argentine side

SIZE 1,696.96km²

ESTABLISHED 1939

UNESCO World Heritage Site since 1986

25°41'S, 54°26'W

Iguaçu National Park
BRAZIL

The roar of the waterfalls drowns out the hissing, buzzing, roaring and screeching sounds of the forest. A trip beyond the colossal Iguaçu Falls in the border region between Argentina and Brazil is well worth it. The park includes various vegetation zones and provides a refuge for many endangered plant and animal species. On the Brazilian side of the falls, the nearly 1,700-square-kilometre national park shelters various wildlife. Parrots and toucans fly among the trees, while swifts nest in the jagged rocks between the waterfalls. Ocelots and jaguars roam alongside tapirs, anteaters and peccaries in the lush rainforest. In the turbulent waters, the once-common giant river otter can still be found hunting for fish.

The wildlife adds vibrant colours to the ever-green rainforest, making it a worthy destination not only for its famous waterfalls but also for its diverse fauna: scarlet ibises, jendaya parakeets, blue-headed parrots (top row, from left), capuchin monkeys (above), crab-eating raccoons, scaly-headed parrots, chestnut-eared aracaris (centre row, from left) and toucans (left).

The Iguaçu Falls, located at the triple border of Brazil, Argentina and Paraguay, are among the largest and most impressive waterfalls in the world. Both the Argentine and Brazilian sides are designated as national parks and have been on the UNESCO World Heritage List since the mid-1980s.

LOCATION Department of Magdalena in northern Colombia; part of the Sierra Nevada de Santa Marta Biosphere Reserve

SIZE 150km^2

ESTABLISHED 1964

Tayrona National Park
COLOMBIA

Like a giant hand with fingers stretching into the water, the foothills of the Sierra Nevada de Santa Marta descend into the sea. Between these green-clad rock fingers lie idyllic coves, snow-white beaches and crystal-clear waters. Coral reefs and mangrove forests run along the coastline. Tropical rainforests and dry forests are also part of Tayrona National Park. Precipitation shapes the landscape, as does the rich diversity of animal and plant life. Over 400 species of birds live here, from the Andean condor to the red-capped woodpecker, while squirrel and capuchin monkeys climb through the trees. Among these is the endangered cotton-top tamarin, which is only found in the tropical forests of northeastern Colombia. This lively species is highly communicative: the sounds it makes almost resemble bird song.

Nature witnesses change over time: rainforests and iguanas existed here long before the region was the tribal land of the Tayrona people.

The cotton-top tamarin (above) is one of the smallest New World money species. It is named after the white crest of hair which runs from its forehead down to its shoulders.

LOCATION Approximately 1,000 kilometres off the west coast of Ecuador
SIZE 140,665.14km^2
ESTABLISHED 1959
UNESCO Biosphere Reserve since 1984
UNESCO World Heritage Site since 1978

Galápagos National Park
ECUADOR

The Galápagos archipelago was born from fire and ash: it comprises more than 100 islands, and a large magma chamber ensures a steady supply. An underground mountain range, known as the Galápagos Ridge, is growing upwards here. At the same time, two tectonic plates are drifting apart: the Nazca Plate and the Cocos Plate. As the Nazca Plate, on which the islands are situated, continues to move eastwards, new islands are formed in the west. In contrast, the oldest, easternmost islands gradually drown as they move downwards with the plate. The westernmost and therefore youngest island is Fernandina and the magma chamber there causes intense volcanic activity. Due to its volcanic origin, the Galápagos archipelago has never been in contact with the mainland. As a result, the flora and fauna, which has developed over millions of years without any external influences, is completely unique.

Not wanting to take a detour, a small lizard simply scurries directly over the foot of a marine iguana (main picture). The latter is endemic to the Galápagos Islands, like many other species, including the Galápagos land iguana (above), red-footed booby, mangrove heron, Galápagos giant tortoise (right, from top), Galápagos sea lion (centre) and great blue heron (opposite).

Right: Bartolomé is one of the smaller islands of the archipelago and is famous for its rock pinnacles; Santiago Island is visible over the turquoise sea.

LOCATION Ancash region, Eastern Peru
LENGTH 180 kilometres

Cordillera Blanca
PERU

The Cordillera Blanca – the "White Mountain Range" – is named for the many glaciers that cloak its peaks in ice and snow. Fifty of these glaciers rise above 5,700 metres, making it the highest mountain range in the Americas. To the west lies the Cordillera Negra – the "Black Mountain Range". The name is fitting, as the area is dominated by dark rock with not a patch of snow in sight. Unfortunately, the Cordillera Blanca is gradually becoming more like the Cordillera Negra, as the glaciers continue to melt, a clear indication of climate change.

The highest tropical mountains in the world are home to Peru's tallest peak, Huascarán, which rises 6,768 metres. The granite of the Cordillera Blanca is covered with snow and ice fields (left).

The impressive mountain scenery of the Cordillera Huayhuash rises in close proximity, challenging climbers with difficult routes (above).

LOCATION Between the western and eastern Andes, stretching across large parts of western Bolivia, Peru, Chile and Argentina

SIZE 170,000km²

Altiplano
BOLIVIA

This broad plateau formed between the western and eastern Andes. A landscape of salt, dry desert sands, ice and fire mountains – the Altiplano spans about 170,000 square kilometres and is one of the largest highlands in the world, second only to Tibet in China. The region has no outlet to the sea, so the lakes here are highly saline due to evaporation. The Altiplano lies at an average altitude of 3,600 metres. Its climate is arid to semi-arid, with average temperatures ranging between two and ten degrees Celsius, whilst snowfall may occur in higher areas between April and September. The plateau is surrounded by active stratovolcanoes which create spectacular sights, such as geysers and hot springs.

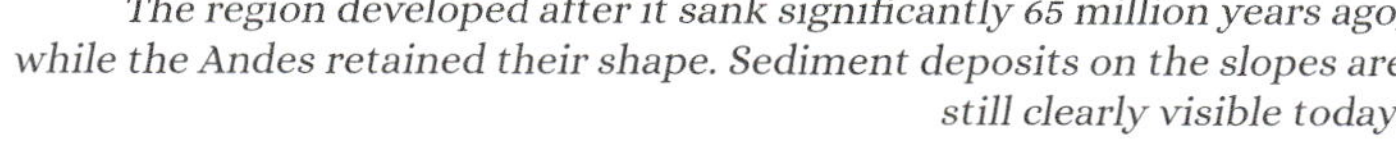

The region developed after it sank significantly 65 million years ago, while the Andes retained their shape. Sediment deposits on the slopes are still clearly visible today.

The vast plains, interspersed with salt flats and mountain ridges, may seem inhospitable at first glance. However, between the colourful stones, large cacti thrive and llamas are commonly found here (above and opposite).

LOCATION West of the Cordillera Occidental, in the far southwest of Bolivia, near the borders with Chile and Argentina
SIZE 7,147km^2
ESTABLISHED 1973

Eduardo Avaroa Andean Fauna National Reserve
BOLIVIA

Hollowed out and wind-blown stones seem casually scattered across an orange sand floor in a landscape that looks like a living Salvador Dalí painting. This desert is one of the main attractions in the Eduardo Avaroa Andean Fauna National Reserve, which is named after a national hero who advanced into Chile during the War of the Pacific. The protected area is framed by the highest mountains of the Andes and includes tourist highlights such as Laguna Colorada and Laguna Blanca. The Laguna Verde, which has an almost Caribbean turquoise hue, is also part of the park, along with the hot springs of Sol de Mañana. Despite the seemingly inhospitable environment, 80 species of birds and 23 species of mammals find food here from the nearly 200 plant species that thrive in the area.

In Laguna Colorada, the park already boasts a stunningly colourful attraction, but it doesn't stop there: Sol de Mañana is as vivid as a living rainbow. Everywhere in this field, steam rises and water boils, thanks to fumaroles, geysers and other geothermal phenomena.

LOCATION Magallanes Region, southern Chile
SIZE 2,420km²
ESTABLISHED 1959
UNESCO Biosphere Reserve since 1978

Torres del Paine National Park
CHILE

The largest glacier area in South America announces itself with a rushing river: the Río Paine carries precious freshwater from the Dickson Glacier through the national park. It flows into the lake of the same name and quickly becomes a raging torrent. Over centuries, it has smoothed rocks and carved channels into them. Its waters tumble down the slopes, delighting hikers and photographers with picturesque waterfalls where, with a bit of luck, you might even spot a rainbow. "Paine" means "sky blue" in the language of the indigenous Tehuelche people, referring to the brilliant turquoise hue of the glacial water. In contrast, the firebush shines bright red when it is in full bloom among the shrub vegetation.

Cerro Paine Grande

The majestically tall mountains shape the morphology of Torres del Paine National Park, which borders the Antarctic region in the far south of Chile. Through the constant flow of glaciers over thousands of years, the granite has been shaped into characteristic peaks and bizarre rock formations, with steep slopes and impressive rock overhangs formed in the stone. The tallest peak is Cerro Paine Grande, which rises into the ever-changing sky, sometimes ice blue, sometimes dramatically red. Although ice and harsh climate dominate the region, large wildfires caused by human negligence have inflicted significant damage on the forest areas. Due to the cold, local plants grow slowly and nature recovers in very small steps.

The first rays of sunlight make the Cuernos del Paine rocks glow. The dark rock caps come from sediments that were pushed to the surface during prehistoric volcanic eruptions (main picture).

Icy winds roar over the hanging Francés Glacier (left). The famous "W" trekking route passes all the natural wonders of this area: from a bird's-eye view, the trail forms the shape of a "W".

LOCATION Northwest Argentina, near San Salvador de Jujuy
SIZE 1,721 km²
UNESCO World Heritage Site since 2003

Quebrada de Humahuaca
ARGENTINA

As if a stone rainbow with its own colour sequence had formed on Earth, the slopes of the 150-kilometre-long Humahuaca Gorge shine in the evening sun in countless shades from citrus yellow to orange, violet, brown, beige, grey and green. In summer, the Río Grande makes its way through the Andean fold, which has been declared a UNESCO World Heritage Site, down into the valley. It winds past small villages like San Francisco de Tilcara with its ancient fortress, the Pucará. For thousands of years, people have used this passage to travel from the highlands to the lowlands. To the west of the colourful Andean slopes, a visit to the Salinas Grandes is well worth the detour: an 800-square-kilometre salt flat at 3,368 metres above sea level. The dazzling white surface, made up of tiny salt crystals, is even accessible by car.

A new day rises sunny and clear over the world-famous Quebrada de Humahuaca. Once, the Incas travelled along this route on their trade path.

The "Hill of Seven Colours", Cerro de los Siete Colores, is formed by different types of rock. According to a legend, however, children sneaked out of their beds at night and painted the mountain in vibrant colours (above and right).

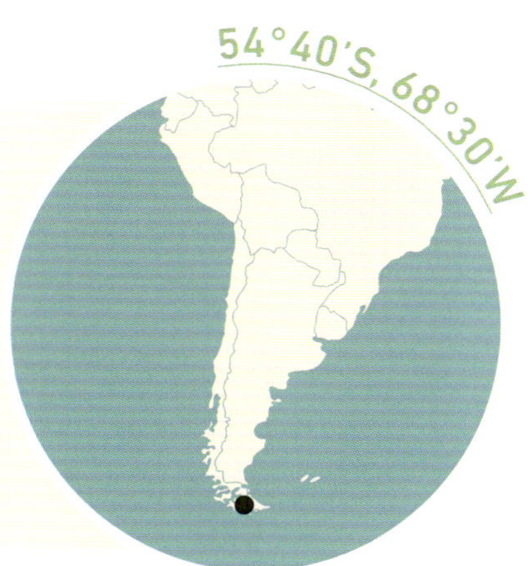

LOCATION Southeastern Tierra del Fuego
SIZE 630km²
ESTABLISHED 1960

Tierra del Fuego National Park
ARGENTINA

The city of Ushuaia is not only a rewarding starting point for a boat tour through the Beagle Channel, but it is also very close to the southernmost national park in Argentina, whose tranquil beauty can be experienced on a ride on the "End of the World" narrow-gauge railway, the "Tren del Fin del Mundo". Peat bogs, lakes such as Lago Roca, the Lapataia Bay, which extends into the park interior from the Beagle Channel, and Andean foothills such as Cerro Guanaco, invite visitors to take solitary hikes, mountain biking trips or canoe rides. There is good provision for such activities, particularly in the southwest of the national park. A notable feature is the remains of a British penal colony that was established at the end of the nineteenth century and lasted until 1941.

The picturesque Ensenada Bay offers park visitors, grass pinks and seabirds a peaceful resting spot (above).

In the coves along the Beagle Channel, waterfowl and sea lions frolic (right).

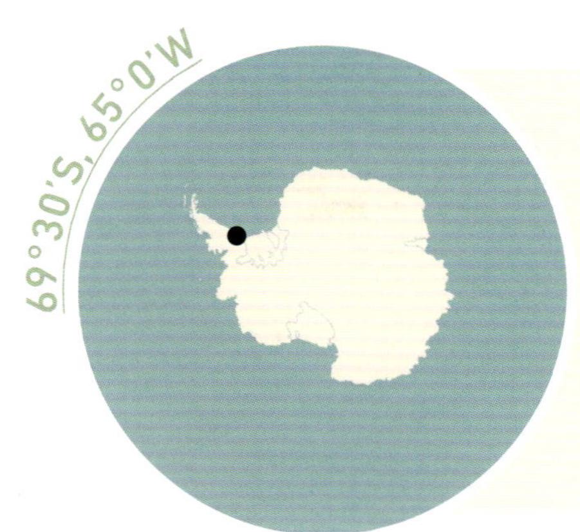

LOCATION Northernmost tip of the Antarctic continent, between Cape Adams and a section south of the Eklund Islands

LENGTH 1,200 kilometres

Antarctic Peninsula
ANTARCTICA

There is nowhere more isolated, inaccessible or lonely than the southernmost continent. Yet, the eternal ice draws not only researchers but also tourists. Most approach by ship from the southern tip of South America, crossing the often stormy Drake Passage to the Antarctic Peninsula, the continent's most accessible point. The roughly 1,200-kilometre-long landmass stretches northward beyond the 65th parallel and fascinates with its fjords, bays and straits, such as the Gerlache Strait. The peninsula is most photogenic in the Lemaire Channel, also known as the "Kodak Channel" because, in the pristine silence, the clicking of cameras is the most audible sound. This six-kilometre-long waterway stretches between the mainland and Booth Island, home to mountains reaching up to 1,000 metres high.

Adélie penguins probably have no sense of the beauty around them (left), while human visitors, on the other hand, perceive the charming allure of the Antarctic Peninsula with awe.

ASIA

40°6'N, 49°23'E

LOCATION Qobustan District in northeastern Azerbaijan, near the Caspian Sea

Mud Volcanoes of Qobustan
AZERBAIJAN

Not all volcanoes spew red-hot fire and molten rock; some are content with water-saturated mud. Nearly a third of the world's approximately 1,100 mud volcanoes are located by the Caspian Sea, on the Absheron Peninsula in Azerbaijan. At regular intervals, around 300 of these cones erupt, throwing hundreds of thousands of cubic kilometres of mud into the barren landscape. Researchers compare this patch of land to Mars, whose surface is also shaped by mud volcanoes. Some of the volcanoes in Azerbaijan even have fire spouts, which are attributed to the presence of methane gas. Since the expelled mud contains iodine, bromine, calcium and magnesium, it is believed to have healing properties and visitors can take a mud bath.

Few animals and plants can be found in the immediate vicinity of the mud volcanoes. However, the Caucasian agama has found a niche for survival here (main picture).

Around 200 eruptions have been recorded here since 1810. The occurrence of mud volcanoes often indicates rich oil deposits beneath the surface.

LOCATION Cappadocia, Central Turkey
SIZE 95.72km²
UNESCO World Heritage Site since 1985

Göreme National Park
TURKEY

It wasn't the Spanish architect Gaudí who shaped these towers, chimneys and mushroom-like formations, but nature. Although they resemble the organic architecture of the great artist of Barcelona, volcanoes were the builders, layering tuff rock over millions of years, with wind and water acting as the stonemasons. Only the harder layers of rock withstood erosion, forming the famous rock formations – the fairy chimneys. From the fourth century onwards, Christian communities in Anatolia sought refuge here and were able to practice their faith undisturbed. They hollowed out the soft tuff rock, creating tunnels, rooms and entire churches. Göreme is the centre of the national park of the same name and is the most accessible of all the valleys, though it is also very touristy. Those seeking seclusion will be more likely to find it in the side valleys.

In the highlands of Nevsehir in Cappadocia, volcanic-origin tuff layers, which rest on older rock, have been eroded to varying degrees. This has created a landscape of mushroom-, pillar- and pyramid-shaped rock formations. Göreme forms the centre of the national park of the same name. The tuff rock keeps the dwellings cool in summer and protects against winter's cold. Some of the cave dwellings have been converted into hotel rooms.

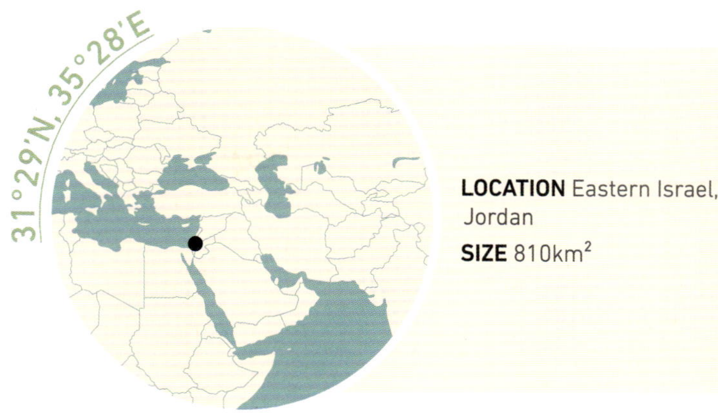

LOCATION Eastern Israel, bordering Jordan
SIZE 810km^2

Dead Sea
ISRAEL

The landlocked Dead Sea is the lowest visible depression in the Earth's crust, lying 428 metres below sea level. Until about 20 years ago, the sea consisted of a larger northern part and a smaller southern part, separated by the Lisan Peninsula. However, the water level has dropped so dramatically that only the northern part remains, with an area of around 800 square kilometres, an average depth of 120 metres and a circumference of 135 kilometres. This is due to the increased water extraction from the Jordan River. Israel and Jordan urgently need this water for irrigation, industry and especially for drinking. However, as evaporation remains high while water input decreases, the Dead Sea is slowly drying up. Since the 1980s, the water level has been sinking by around one metre per year.

The Dead Sea is fed by the Jordan River, which holds particular significance in Christian belief as the site of Jesus' baptism. The river transports fresh water into the sea, which then becomes salty due to evaporation.

Natural water basins near the Dead Sea collect water, which evaporates in the intense sunlight, leaving behind a thick salt crust (top left).

LOCATION Southern Jordan, on the border with Saudi Arabia
SIZE 740km^2
UNESCO World Heritage Site since 2011

Wadi Rum Nature Reserve
JORDAN

Located on a sandstone plateau, Wadi Rum was formed about 30 million years ago as a result of a geological fault, where a large crack in the earth opened up vast canyons and isolated individual mountains. Over millions of years, erosion shaped the area into a spectacular desert landscape with narrow gorges, bizarre rock formations and numerous caves. The mountains surrounding Wadi Rum are made of granite and sandstone. The darker granite forms the base, while the reddish sandstone forms the peaks. This also explains the many springs found particularly in the narrower parts of the desert valley: rainwater from winter precipitation seeps through the porous sandstone, hits the impermeable granite and flows downhill, where the springs often emerge dozens of metres above the valley floor.

The numerous springs in Wadi Rum help to explain the early settlement of the valley in the Neolithic period (10,000 to 6,000 BC). Wadi Rum became famous largely through the accounts of Lawrence of Arabia, who wrote in his book The Seven Pillars of Wisdom: "...one felt frightened and ashamed to set up camp in the midst of these colossal mountains".

LOCATION The Pamir mountain range spans Kyrgyzstan, China, Afghanistan and Tajikistan
SIZE 120,000km^2

Pamir Mountains
TAJIKISTAN

The second-highest mountain range on Earth spans four countries (Kyrgyzstan, China, Afghanistan and Tajikistan) and, like the Himalayas, is part of the "Roof of the World". However, compared to the Himalayas, it is still largely undeveloped for tourism. The Pamir Mountains form the junction of the highest mountain chains on the Eurasian continent (the Tian Shan, the Karakoram, the Kunlun Shan and the Hindu Kush), and are home to the longest glacier outside the polar regions. They are also very active geologically. Around 100 years ago, an earthquake led to the formation of the deep blue Sarez Lake: a massive landslide buried the village of Usoi and completely blocked the valley. The largest lake in the Pamir Mountains, Karakul, formed around five million years ago from a meteorite crater. Despite the extreme temperature fluctuations between day and night, and across seasons, the Pamir Mountains support a rich alpine flora, mostly of Central Asian origin.

Crystal-clear waters, some fed by glaciers and reflecting the sky's blue, provide a striking contrast to the jagged brown-grey rocks of the rugged mountain massif.

LOCATION Ömnögovi Province, southern Mongolia
SIZE 27,000km^2
ESTABLISHED 1993

Gobi Gurvansaikhan National Park
MONGOLIA

Part of the Gobi Gurvansaikhan National Park, Khongoryn Els is probably the most spectacular sight in the Gobi Desert. The largest sand dunes in Mongolia are famous for their "Singing Dunes". When the wind blows over the summit at a certain angle, the sliding sand produces an organ-like whistle that can be heard for miles. Because the wind always blows from north to south, the dunes can reach heights of up to 300 metres. Those who try to climb a dune will realize the incredible capabilities of camels as transport on sand. In the north, parallel to the dunes, lush vegetation lines the Khongoryn Gol. Fed by underground sources, this river flows alongside the sand dunes and forms an oasis in the dry landscape.

Khongoryn Els is an 80-kilometre-long dune field in a narrow valley in the Gobi-Altai Mountains. With temperatures ranging from -15 degrees Celsius in January to 20 degrees Celsius in July, these mega-dunes rise to more than 300 metres. Due to their striking pale yellow colour, the dunes radiate a unique calm, although this tranquillity is broken when the wind sweeps over the peaks and produces sounds that can be heard for miles. The dunes are surrounded by steppe as far as the eye can see.

LOCATION The Chinese part of the mountain range is located in the northwest of the Xinjiang autonomous region

SIZE 6,068.33km²

UNESCO World Heritage Site since 2013

Tian Shan
CHINA

A gigantic ocean must once have existed here, at the northern foothills of the Tian Shan: the Kuitun Canyon, near the towns of Dushanzi and Wusu, was not formed by rivers like other famous canyons of the world. Part of the Xinjiang Tian Shan UNESCO World Heritage Site, the Kuitun Canyon is composed entirely of sand and gravel from a seabed that was eroded over millions of years, creating a solid mountain landscape with numerous crevices and fissures. Geological processes further shaped the canyon into its current form. The vast canyon system is crossed by many streams and rivers from the Tian Shan, whose watercourses change depending on the season and rainfall.

Few are left unimpressed by the view of Kuitun Canyon. In spring, the waters swell and flow around the canyon's rock walls, shaped by deep fissures.

LOCATION Central southern Chongqing, part of the South China Karst.

UNESCO World Heritage Site since 2007

Wulong Karst
CHINA

In tropical South China, weathering resulting from carbonic acid reactions have led to the creation of distinctive karst landscapes. The intense weathering in this region has produced fantastic formations, such as cone-shaped karst, tower karst and stone forests. The South China Karst UNESCO World Heritage Site encompasses several areas with correspondingly named formations: the Shilin Karst, near Kunming; the Libo Karst, near Guiyang; and the Wulong Karst, near Chongqing. The Wulong Karst also includes an area known as the "Three Natural Bridges" – enduring stone bridges formed through karst erosion. The bridges are named after dragons in Chinese: Tianlong (Heavenly Dragon), Qinglong (Azure Dragon) and Heilong (Black Dragon), and are surrounded by canyons, caves and waterfalls.

Conventions are absent here, as no view is the same as the next. However, they do share one thing in common: the karst formations are impressive, whether covered in greenery or forming natural gates. Water, fortunately, has no fear, as it plunges freely, falling about 80 metres from rock edges into narrow gorges.

The mandarin snake, with its colourful spots, is not exactly inconspicuous. However, it compensates for this disadvantage with its speed.

LOCATION Directly north of the city of Zhangjiajie, northwest Hunan; part of the Zhangjiajie Global Geopark

SIZE 264km²

UNESCO World Heritage Site since 1992

Wulingyuan Scenic and Historic Interest Area
CHINA

The sandstone peaks of this spectacular area in Hunan Province, southeast China, were formed from a 500-metre-thick layer of sediment through the forces of erosion. The valleys between them are so narrow that no agriculture is possible, leaving the region largely uninhabited. Many of the most prominent rock formations have evocative names and lie within an area of dense vegetation intersected by streams. Around 3,000 plant species have been counted here and the air is generally very humid. Among the other notable attractions of this landscape are two natural bridges – one is 26 metres long and located about 100 metres above the valley floor, while the other, more spectacular, bridge is 40 metres long and sits approximately 350 metres above the valley floor.

"Mystical" is perhaps the word that best describes the impression made by the dark green-covered sandstone and karst formations, especially when dense fog clings to their feet.

Like solitary giants frozen in stone for eternity, the columns rise into the sky. Rhesus monkeys live among the rocks here (above).

LOCATION In western Gansu Province; to the east of the park lies the city of Zhangye
SIZE 322km^2
ESTABLISHED 2012

Zhangye Danxia Geopark
CHINA

Some landscapes seem so surreal that it's easy to believe humans had a hand in creating them. This impression is especially strong in the Zhangye Danxia Geopark, where a vast expanse of mountain slopes appears as though an artist had painted multicoloured stripes with giant pastel crayons. However, the rainbow colours of the mountains are entirely natural. Over millions of years, the once-red sandstone has been eroded and the underlying rock layers exposed. Combined with the desert climate, harsh frost and wind, a unique structure has formed here. Like perfect lines in a drawing, the coloured sediment layers stretch for miles through the landscape. Shuttle buses travel back and forth between the sights.

These colourful rock formations in the Chinese Zhangye Danxia Geopark are also called the "Rainbow Mountains". They offer a colour palette that initially looks unreal. But the colouring of the sandstone is, in fact, a charming quirk of nature – not a result of chemicals or any toxic waste from civilization.

35°52'N, 129°13'E

LOCATION North Gyeongsang Province, eastern South Korea; the nearest city is Gyeongju

SIZE 138km²

ESTABLISHED 1968

UNESCO World Heritage Site since 2000

Gyeongju National Park
SOUTH KOREA

A beautiful wilderness combines with ancient cultural treasures in Gyeongju National Park. As Korea's only historical national park, it caters to both nature and culture lovers alike. The painted wooden doors at the Mangwolsa Temple are as impressive as the markings of a local venomous tiger snake, which hikers should avoid being bitten by. Natural rock weathering forms patterns alongside Buddha figures carved into granite stone. The park's landmark is the famous Bulguksa Temple, which has stood in place for nearly 1,500 years, although no stone remains from the ancient Silla era. Nature enthusiasts will also find Japanese red pines here, and the mandarin duck, which is prized for its colourful plumage.

There are times when it seems like trees are secretly dancing, though normally, they go unnoticed by humans – much less photographed, like these sacred pines in the park.

Here, you may encounter hoopoes (above), chipmunks and Mandarin ducks (opposite).

LOCATION Northern Hokkaidō, Japan's main island
SIZE 386km²
ESTABLISHED 1964
UNESCO World Natural Heritage Site since 2005

44°9'N, 145°14'E

Shiretoko National Park
JAPAN

Cold winds from Siberia cause the sea to freeze further south here than anywhere else in the Northern Hemisphere. Beneath the ice layer, large amounts of phytoplankton develop, forming the base of a long food chain. This phytoplankton serves as the primary food source for krill and other tiny aquatic creatures. These, in turn, sustain seals, sea lions and sea eagles. Salmon and trout swim upstream into the interior to spawn, providing food for brown bears and the critically endangered Blakiston's fish owl, as well as Steller's sea eagles. Off the coast of Shiretoko National Park, 223 species of fish and 28 marine mammals have been recorded. The Steller sea lion, part of the eared seal family, requires special protection. Shellfish and small fish, which are consumed by larger fish and marine mammals, play an important role in the region's complex ecosystem.

The Shiretoko National Park invites visitors to relax and unwind with its tranquil lakes and rushing waterfalls. Yezo sika deer (above), a subspecies of the sika deer, can be found in the interior of the park.

A Steller's sea eagle swiftly snatches its prey from the water (left).

LOCATION Central Honshu; the park includes Mount Fuji, the Fuji Five Lakes, Hakone, the Izu Peninsula and islands

SIZE 1,218km²

ESTABLISHED 1936

Fuji-Hakone-Izu National Park
JAPAN

Mount Fuji, part of the Fuji-Hakone-Izu National Park, is not just a sacred mountain, it is a god. It is considered to be the heart of the Japanese people. When they feel sad, they just have to look at Mount Fuji and they are instantly comforted. Mount Fuji is also a miraculous mountain. It is believed that those who climb it become better people, as they share in its divine perfection on its snow-capped peak. That is why every year, hundreds of thousands of pilgrims journey to the 3,776-metre-high peak, which stands as an awe-inspiring solitary mountain on Honshu. No other mountain dares to compete with it – only a god could have such stature. But there is no room for reverence at Mount Fuji during the official climbing season, which lasts only two months, beginning on July 1st. During this time, the world flocks to the mountain.

It is the symbol of Japan and the essence of the Japanese soul: standing at 3,776 metres, Mount Fuji is not only the highest mountain in Japan but the most famous by far. Today, the stratovolcano is as much a spiritual place as it is a tourist attraction. It is often forgotten that Mount Fuji is still active and could erupt at any time.

LOCATION In the Sobo-Katamuki-Okue mountain range, Kyushu
SIZE 2,436km²
UNESCO Biosphere Reserve since 2017

Sobo, Katamuki and Okue Biosphere Reserve
JAPAN

Forest, forest and more forest: the area around the three mountains Sobo, Katamuki and Okue, designated a biosphere reserve in 2017, is almost entirely covered by trees. Mainly beech trees, with evergreen conifers in the higher elevations, form a dense green canopy from above, home to species like the Sika deer. Solitary hikes are easily possible in this relatively underdeveloped tourist area, with a sufficiently developed network of trails. Sobo, the highest mountain in the reserve, stands at 1,756 metres. The Okue mountain area also offers exciting landscapes. The region was designated a biosphere reserve to honour and strengthen the interplay between humans, nature and traditional craftsmanship, including activities such as shiitake mushroom cultivation, forest management and charcoal production.

The Manai Waterfalls in the Takachiho Gorge are 17 metres high. The contrast of the waterfall against the lush green slopes is truly impressive (main picture).

The water of the Takachiho Gorge carves its way through narrow rock crevices and over moss-covered boulders (above).

LOCATION West of the Hindukush mountain range and south of the Himalayas, the Karakoram mountain range stretches across the disputed borders of Pakistan, India and China

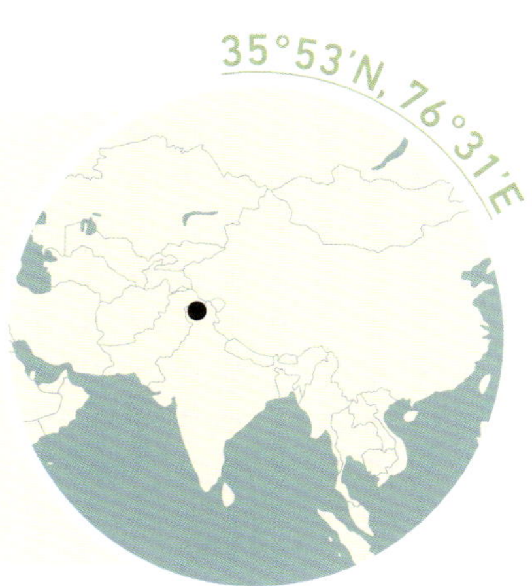

Karakorum
PAKISTAN

Around 1,500 years ago, the Chinese pilgrim Faxian, in search of Buddhist holy sites, traversed the deepest depths and the most towering heights of the Himalayas. One day, he reached the Karakorum and froze in shock and awe. The mountains, he later wrote, were "a wall of stone rising 10,000 feet above the Indus". Even today, one stands frozen before the Karakorum, which rises abruptly up to 5,500 metres from the plain, as if it were the fortress wall of the sky, crowned by K2, the second-highest mountain on Earth. The Himalayas are nowhere as rough and jagged as the Karakorum and the wildness of nature is reflected in the people. It is a world beyond the world, where progress came very late – so late that the residents are said to have offered hay as feed when the first jeeps appeared in the Karakorum.

Those taking the long path to the summit of K2 will likely pass this snow-covered scree field, known as Ali Camp, located just before the Gondogoro Pass (right). The Laila Peak is also a notable sight (above).

LOCATION Northwestern Nepal, bordering Tibet in China to the north

SIZE 1,148km^2

ESTABLISHED 1976

UNESCO World Heritage Site since 1979

snp.gov.np

Sagarmatha National Park
NEPAL

The popular trekking region at the foot of the world's highest mountain – 8,848-metre-high Mount Everest – is full of fascinating alpine flora and fauna. However, the impact of trekking and its infrastructure has led to problems in the Himalayas. To stabilize the ecological balance around Mount Everest, the area was designated a National Park in 1976. The highest mountain on Earth is known as Sagarmatha, or "Goddess of the Sky" in Nepali, while the Tibetans call it Chomolungma, or "Goddess Mother of the Earth". The region around Sagarmatha National Park is the highest mountainous area on Earth, housing three eight-thousanders – Mount Everest, Lhotse and Cho Oyu – as well as additional six- and seven-thousanders. The park is home to 30 mammal species, although, despite all the legends, no Yeti has been officially recorded.

Above: for a short period in summer, the southern slopes of the mountain giants are free of snow, revealing a rich diversity of flora and fauna. Mount Everest is seen on the left of the picture and Nuptse, towering at 7,861 metres, is visible on the right.

Right: the view of Mount Everest is even more spectacular from Kala Patthar (5,545 metres), which can be reached by a hike from base camp.

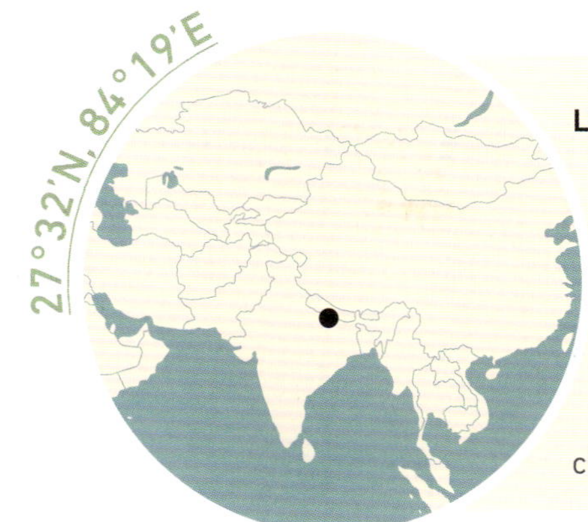

LOCATION Southern Nepal, about five hours by car from Kathmandu; around the popular destination, there are jungle lodges and hotels

SIZE 932km²

ESTABLISHED 1973

UNESCO World Heritage Site since 1984

chitwannationalpark.gov.np

Chitwan National Park
NEPAL

As Nepal's oldest national park, with its sal forests and vast elephant grasslands, Chitwan National Park is home to numerous endangered species. One will undoubtedly encounter one of the 400 Indian rhinoceroses that live here. An adult rhino can consume up to 200 kilograms of grass and drink up to 100 litres of water per day. The park is also home to about 200 leopards and 80 tigers, which roam the tall grasses. The park owes its existence to King Mahendra, who founded a conservation area for the endangered species of rhinoceroses in 1962. The reserve was declared a national park in 1973.

Common wild species found here include sambar and axis deer, four-horned antelopes, wild boars, sloth bears, wild cattle (gaur), rhesus monkeys and gharials. The treetops are populated by langurs and at dusk, mongooses and honey badgers can be spotted hunting.

Despite its sluggish appearance, the Indian rhinoceros, weighing up to two tons, can reach speeds of 45 km/h when angered. When this happens, it's best to be far away! At night, the eerie howls of golden jackals can be heard and in the open terrain, one may also encounter Bengal monitors. Tigers are rare but are sometimes spotted, while red deer are more common.

In the park's rivers, you can spot mugger crocodiles and gharials with their distinct long snouts (above). Gharials, a member of the crocodile family, once inhabited all the major rivers of the northern Indian subcontinent. However, their population has dwindled drastically, with an estimated 95 percent decline in the last 70 years, according to the International Union for Conservation of Nature (IUCN).

LOCATION In the central-eastern part of Jammu-Kashmir, in the Ladakh region

SIZE 4,400km²

ESTABLISHED 1981

Hemis National Park
INDIA

Every twelve years, a vibrant and joyous festival is held at the Hemis Monastery in Ladakh, celebrating the Year of the Monkey, which is seen as an omen of great fortune. The monastery, one of the largest and oldest in the region, is located about 40 kilometres from Leh, surrounded by the Hemis National Park. With an elevation of over 3,000 metres, the park offers a unique habitat, particularly for the rare snow leopard, with an estimated 50 leopards residing in the area. The region's pine forests are well-suited to the dry climate, creating a stunning landscape that blends majestic rock formations, deep gorges and flowing rivers. This remote, rugged environment transports visitors back in time, far from the conveniences of modern life.

Bearded vultures, known for their small heads, shaggy neck feathers and wide wingspan, soar through the skies here. The view from above encompasses jagged peaks and turquoise river valleys (above).

Despite the harsh conditions, wildlife thrives in this barren yet beautiful terrain, including goats and the endangered Ladakh urial (right), which navigate this rugged landscape with ease.

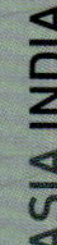

LOCATION Eastern Rajasthan, near Leh, in the Ladakh region
SIZE 282km^2
ESTABLISHED 1980

Ranthambore National Park
INDIA

In the deep, enigmatic eyes of a royal Bengal tiger, time seems to stand still. During an encounter, the difference between human and animal vanishes for what feels like eternity. It's as if a silent, unspoken question is exchanged in the tiger's gaze, with the answer remaining solely with the majestic predator. The tiger, one of the most regal of creatures, prowls in the vast expanses of the Ranthambore National Park, a protected area spanning nearly 300 square kilometres. Here, the tiger can roam freely, far from the threat of poachers, preserving its sovereignty in the wild. The park offers sanctuary for other predators like sloth bears, golden jackals and honey badgers, as well as prey species such as four-horned antelopes, sambar deer and Indian gazelles. This ecosystem, once vast, has been reduced by human encroachment and deforestation, leaving protected areas like Ranthambore critical for the tiger's survival.

Despite the modern world's reach, Ranthambore's mystical aura remains untarnished, especially when a royal tiger yawns or tenderly plays with its cubs – moments that embody the untamed spirit of nature.

LOCATION Approximately 150 kilometres northwest of Malé, north of the Kashidhoo-Kandhoo Canal

SIZE 1,200km^2

ESTABLISHED 1998

UNESCO World Heritage Site since 2011

Baa Atoll Biosphere Reserve
MALDIVES

The Baa Atoll Biosphere Reserve spans 1,200 square kilometres and consists of 75 islands, 13 of which are inhabited by around 12,000 people. Located approximately 150 kilometres north of the capital island Malé, the atoll is especially active in the summer months when large amounts of plankton drift into the area, attracting schools of manta rays. These majestic creatures, with a wingspan of nearly four metres, glide through the lagoons around Kihavah and the nearby island of Landaa Giraavaru, offering an unforgettable experience for divers. Despite their large size and wide-open mouths, mantas are gentle and peaceful, circling divers with graceful wingbeats that resemble an eagle's flight before disappearing into the deep blue.

The atoll's coral reefs and mangrove forests have tremendous ecological significance, as they support an extraordinarily high level of biodiversity, even by Maldivian standards. In addition to manta rays, turtles, tropical fish, whale sharks and napoleon wrasse thrive in the vibrant coral ecosystems, making this region a unique haven for marine life.

LOCATION Southeastern Sri Lanka, near the town of Tissamaharama

SIZE 1,500km^2

ESTABLISHED 1938

Yala National Park
SRI LANKA

Yala, the oldest national park in Sri Lanka, was established in 1938, though the area was protected from as early as 1899. It lies in the southeastern region of the island and is divided into Yala West and Yala East. Once known as Ruhuna, after the kingdom it once belonged to, this park offers diverse ecosystems, including savannahs and monsoon forests, making it a rich habitat for a wide variety of species. Among the park's most notable inhabitants are the Sri Lankan leopard and elephants, sloth bears and the Indian langur, a slender monkey. However, it is the blue peacock, with its stunningly vibrant plumage, that often steals the show. The park is also home to sambar deer, axis deer and the strikingly colourful red-faced malkoha, a species of cuckoo, which can often be spotted in the treetops.

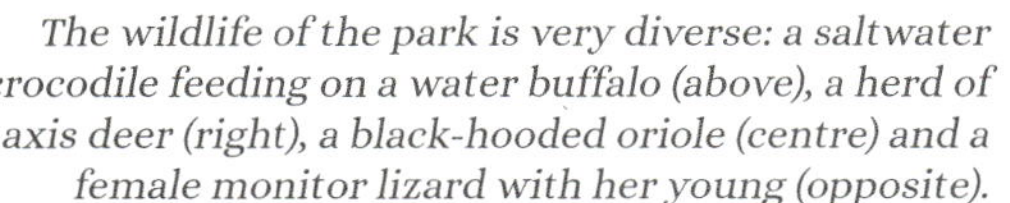

The wildlife of the park is very diverse: a saltwater crocodile feeding on a water buffalo (above), a herd of axis deer (right), a black-hooded oriole (centre) and a female monitor lizard with her young (opposite).

LOCATION Ubon Ratchathani Province, northeastern Thailand

Sam Phan Bok
THAILAND

The scenery at Sam Phan Bok appears as if it's from another planet. Here, the Mekong River has become an artist, making extensive use of nature's palette of shapes and colours. It has smoothed corners and carved rocks with marvellous holes, where the water creates beautiful plays of colour and light – from turquoise to almost black, the colours are extraordinary. In many of these pools, new life has formed in the form of water lilies that add a fresh green accent to the scene. Some visitors compare the orange tones and polished rocks to the canyons of the western USA, which is why this natural park is also known as the "Grand Canyon of Thailand".

The mighty Mekong has gnawed over 3,000 holes into the rocks at Sam Phan Bok. Some are small, while others are as large as ponds. A visit here feels like a dazzling celebration of colours, but it's only possible during the dry season from January to April, as the area is otherwise inaccessible. The rest of the year, this wonderland is completely submerged in water.

LOCATION In the Andaman Sea, off the southwest coast of Thailand, Phang-Nga Province
SIZE 140km²
ESTABLISHED 1982

Mu Ko Similan National Park
THAILAND

Like a string of pearls, the nine islands of the Similan Islands lie 70 kilometres off the western coast of Thailand in the Andaman Sea. For simplicity, they are numbered from north to south. Together with two additional islands, they form the Mu Ko Similan National Park, which is part of Phang-Nga Province. Divers and snorkellers enjoy spectacular visibility, usually ranging from 18 to 25 metres, sometimes even exceeding 40 metres underwater. The dive sites on the western side of the islands are open to the sea, while those on the eastern side are bordered by coral reefs. Larger species of wildlife around the Similan Islands include whale sharks, stingrays, grey reef sharks and manta rays. On land, idyllic beaches with fine, white sand attract visitors. The islands are also known for their towering rock formations, some reaching heights of up to 200 metres.

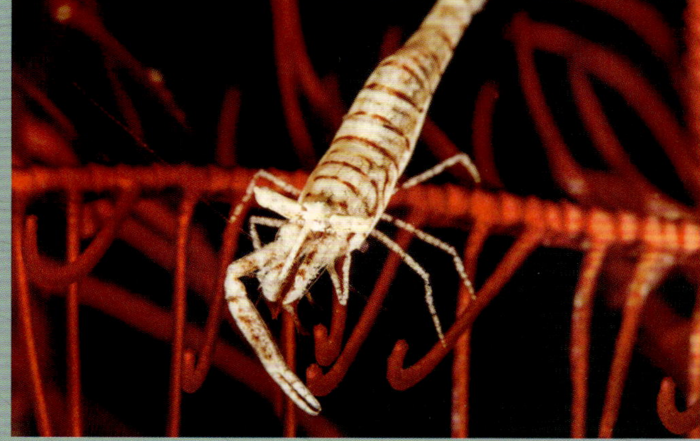

The Similan Islands are the ideal place for an underwater adventure: the dive sites of the Mu Ko Similan National Park are among the best in the world.

Divers and snorkellers in this underwater paradise will encounter bluestripe snapper and redtail butterflyfish (opposite top), along with spotfin lionfish, bluestripe pygmygoby and crinoid shrimp (left, from top).

LOCATION Phang-Nga Province, southern Thailand
SIZE 401km²
ESTABLISHED 1981

Ao Phang-Nga National Park
THAILAND

Like the backs of prehistoric dragons, bizarre island peaks, cones and pyramids rise out of the water in Phang-Nga Bay: the visible remnants of a limestone reef that formed over 100 million years ago in the Andaman Sea and once stretched from northern Malaysia to central China. In 1981, an area of about 400 square kilometres was designated as the Ao Phang-Nga National Park. The park aims to protect the mangrove forests in the northern part of the bay, the largest of their kind in Thailand. One of the most famous rock formations is Khao Tapu, also known as "Nail Island", which, according to legend, is the half of a needle that an angry fisherman, frustrated by repeatedly catching it in his net instead of fish, threw back into the sea. Many islands in the park contain karst caves, which may have been used as shelters since prehistoric times.

The bay is about 50 kilometres long and wide, with no dangerous currents and it opens into the open sea to the south. A magical world of stone can be found in the many limestone caves.

The most iconic rock is the so-called Nail Island: Khao Tapu. In the James Bond film The Man with the Golden Gun (1974), this island served as the antenna that threatened the world (right).

LOCATION Cao Bang Province, northern Vietnam, on the border with China

Ban Gioc-Detian Falls
VIETNAM

Located on the border with China, the Ban Gioc-Detian Falls are situated in northern Vietnam, making them part of a long list of transboundary waterfalls. They are the fourth largest waterfalls in the world (after Iguaçu, Victoria and Niagara). The Quy Xuan River cascades over multiple levels, falling 53 metres across a width of 300 metres. During the rainy season from May to September, a continuous water curtain forms, while during the rest of the year, it divides into several cascades. The waterfalls are surrounded by rice paddies and towering karst peaks, which contribute to the scenic beauty of the region. Directly nearby, on the Chinese side, lies the kilometre-long Tongling Grand Canyon, which is accessible only through a cave passage. Some recently discovered endemic plant species can be found here.

The water has to overcome many different levels before it can flow into a plunge pool at the base of the falls. The area surrounding the waterfalls is covered with lush, green rainforest that provides a habitat for many rare plants.

LOCATION In the Gulf of Tonkin, Quang Ninh Province, northern Vietnam

SIZE 1,500km^2

UNESCO World Heritage Site since 1994

Halong Bay
VIETNAM

The rocks in Halong Bay are distinguished by their great variety of forms, ranging from pyramids with broad bases to highly vaulted "elephant backs" and slender needles. People have viewed the island landscape not just as a natural phenomenon, but as a mythical spectacle: a "descending dragon" (Ha Long) is said to have created the natural wonder when he destroyed an enemy army with the blows of his mighty tail – or perhaps he was merely driven by rage after being disturbed? The water then flooded the furrows formed by the dragon as he dived into the sea. The geological explanation is more straightforward: after the last ice age, the coastal landscape, part of the south-western Chinese limestone plateau, sank and was flooded by water. Erosion shaped the rock into bizarre cones.

The peculiar island landscape of the Gulf of Tonkin consists of around 2,000 islands and limestone cliffs. Wind, weather and tides have together created a graceful masterpiece of nature. The karst rocks, some rising up to 100 metres above the water, are densely covered with vegetation and resemble traditional Chinese landscape paintings.

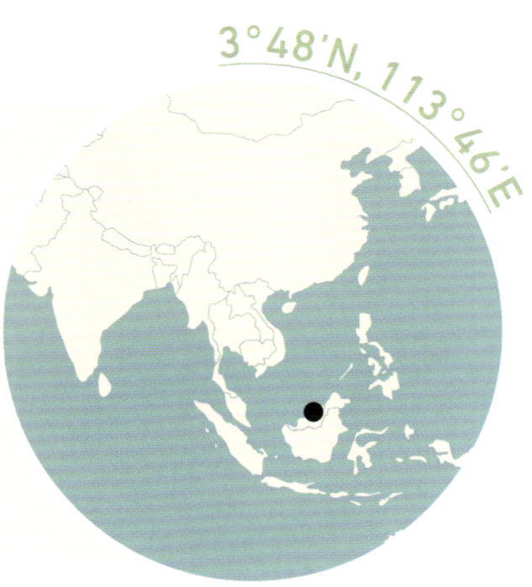

LOCATION On the northern coast of Borneo, near the town of Niah

SIZE 31.4km²

ESTABLISHED 1974

UNESCO World Heritage Site since 2024

Niah National Park
MALAYSIA

This area was inhabited by modern humans as far back as 45,000 years ago, as evidenced by the discovery of skull fragments from a *Homo sapiens* in the Late Pleistocene, which was found in the Niah Caves in 1958. These are the earliest evidence of *Homo sapiens*' presence on the islands of the Malay Archipelago. The vast cave passages of the national park are still far from fully explored and, so far, tools, jewellery and 1,200-year-old rock paintings have been discovered. A large colony of swiflets lives in the caves. These birds build their nests out of their saliva, which is considered a delicacy in China and used as a key ingredient in bird's nest soup. Local Penang people harvest these nests and sell them for export at high prices.

The park holds a certain mystical quality, thanks in part to the mysterious caves and the dense green vegetation that barely allows sunlight to pass through, but does allow mist to rise. As beautiful as the caves of Borneo are, some of the inhabitants can be quite frightening when unexpectedly encountered, like this large cave cricket (above).

LOCATION Spanning the states of Kelantan, Pahang and Terengganu in the northern part of the Malay Peninsula

SIZE 4,343km²

ESTABLISHED 1938/39

Taman Negara National Park
MALAYSIA

Taman Negara, the national park in the northern part of the Malay Peninsula, is home to an extensive primeval tropical rainforest, making it the oldest forest area on Earth at 130 million years old. While many parts of the world have changed due to ice ages, climate fluctuations and sea level changes, the conditions on the Malay Peninsula have remained relatively stable, allowing flora and fauna to develop almost undisturbed. The Taman Negara rainforest is home to Asian elephants, panthers, Malayan tapirs, wild boars, monkeys and endangered species like the Malayan tiger and Sumatran rhinoceros. There are over a thousand butterfly species and over 600 bird species native to this area. The climate is tropical year-round, with especially high humidity.

A look around the forests of Taman Negara National Park reveals magnificent feathered specimens, including the scarlet-rumped trogon (main picture) and the milky stork (above).

Top row, from left to right: Diard's trogon and crow pheasant.

Centre row, from left to right: Malayan crested fireback and crimson-winged woodpecker.

Bottom row, from left to right: chestnut-rumped babbler, chestnut-breasted malkoha, black-bellied malkoha and green broadbill.

LOCATION Bicol region, southeastern Luzon
SIZE 58.03km^2
ESTABLISHED 2000

Mayon Volcano Natural Park
PHILIPPINES

At the southern tip of the island of Luzon lies a unique protected area: in the mix of grassland and rainforest, more than 180 plant species have settled, 46 of which are endemic. The mangrove forest, in particular, is very species-rich and is a true paradise for birds. The Luzon bleeding-heart dove, a bird found only in this region, always surprises nature watchers due to the red spot on its chest, which resembles a heart pierced by a dart. Conversely, the bright green Philippine pit vipers, which love to climb trees, often evoke more fear than sympathy. Ancient cultures of indigenous groups are still present on the slopes of Mount Mayon and many people make a living from traditional crafts such as weaving, pottery and hemp processing. However, due to climate change, the region is frequently affected by landslides and heavy rainfall.

A model example of a volcano: Mayon rises almost perfectly conical into the sky, topped with a small plume of smoke (main picture). The same cone shape can also be found in the Quitinday Green Hills (above).

Mount Mayon demonstrates how ambivalent nature can be: as dangerous and disturbing as any volcanic eruption is, the sight of glowing lava reflected in the water at dusk can also be beautiful. The upper part of the fire mountain features steep slopes of 35 to 40 degrees, with a relatively small crater at the summit.

LOCATION Bicol region, southeastern Luzon
HEIGHT 2,462 metres

Mayon

On the Bicol Peninsula in the southeast of Luzon, the approximately 2,460-metre-high stratovolcano Mayon rises. It is considered one of the most beautiful volcanoes in the world due to its well-formed shape, but it is also infamous for its sudden eruptions, often accompanied by pyroclastic flows and lahars. The second-highest volcano in the Philippines is also one of the most active volcanoes in the island nation and has erupted over 45 times since the first recorded eruption in 1616. Located in a densely populated area, every eruption poses a serious danger to the nearby towns and villages, illustrated by the most devastating eruption in 1814, which claimed more than 1,200 lives. The wonderfully symmetrical stratovolcano has a base circumference of 20 kilometres and an almost circular shape when viewed from the air.

3°34'N, 97°37'E

LOCATION In the extreme northwest of Sumatra

SIZE 9,000km^2

ESTABLISHED 1980

UNESCO Biosphere Reserve since 1981

UNESCO World Natural Heritage Site since 2004

Gunung Leuser National Park
INDONESIA

In Sumatra, the pressure of the growing population is so immense that vast areas of rainforest are being burned to make room for fields and palm oil plantations. Covering an area of 9,000 square kilometres in the north of the island, Gunung Leuser National Park is one of Indonesia's largest protected areas. It is not only a safe haven for rare monkeys, but also one of Indonesia's most important wilderness areas. There is little remaining habitat in Indonesia for orangutans and other wildlife, such as tigers and rhinoceroses, but in this refuge, notable populations of highly endangered animals, such as the Sumatran rhinoceros and the Sumatran tiger, still exist. They live in a world of unimaginable biodiversity, with up to 130 different species of trees growing on just a single hectare.

The national park is renowned for its rich wildlife. The Sumatran elephants (main picture) are endemic to this area and are considered an endangered species.

Here, in the north of Sumatra, endangered orangutans are left in peace (middle right). This protection also benefits the Javan macaques (above) and the southern pig-tailed macaques (top right).

The flower of the red Rafflesia can reach a diametre of up to one metre when in full bloom (right).

LOCATION SoutheasternJava
ELEVATION 3,670 metres (Semeru)

Java's Fire Mountains

Nothing reveals the wonders concealed by the night and veiled in darkness. Nothing gives the visitors a hint of what they will soon witness when they ascend to the Fire Mountains of Surabaya in eastern Java. As the pitch-black night slowly fades away, it reveals the outlines of three gigantic mountains. They become clearer and sharper, gradually peeling away from the darkness. And suddenly, they stand before you, surreal and threatening like emissaries from hell: the dormant Batok volcano, looking like the home of a monster mole; the hyperactive Bromo behind it, with its sizzling crater and stinking sulfur breath; and the majestic Semeru, from whose summit a column of smoke rises as if giants were sitting around a fireplace inside.

LOCATION Southeastern Java
AREA 413,374km^2
ESTABLISHED 1982
UNESCO Biosphere Reserve since 2015

Bromo Tengger Semeru National Park
INDONESIA

One of the most famous national parks in Indonesia has been expanded into a biosphere reserve: among all the volcanoes of Java, the 2,392-metre-high Gunung Bromo is the most visited thanks to its unique setting. The volcanic cone and the surrounding mountainous landscape with its steep slopes are easily accessible. Nearby stands Semeru, the highest volcano on Java, towering at 3,676 metres. Climbing this mountain, surrounded by picturesque alpine lakes, is no easy feat: you must ascend 1,300 metres, with half of the route traversing open, steep lava debris below the crater. This isolated mountain region is home to the Tengger people. As Islam spread across Java, the indigenous population retreated into the mountains, where they have managed to preserve their Hindu traditions to this day.

It is the most spectacular landscape panorama in Indonesia – and one of the most fleeting, as the volcanoes often veil themselves in clouds, leaving visitors with the feeling they may have only dreamed of it.

Black lava forms vast dune fields at the edge of Bromo, which regularly experiences minor eruptions. Most of its eruptions are of the strombolian type, where ash, lapilli (walnut-sized lava fragments), slag and bombs (hardened lava fragments) are ejected in short bursts and relatively weak surges.

AUSTRALIA & OCEANIA

LOCATION Off the east coast of Queensland

SIZE 348,700km²

UNESCO World Heritage Site since 1981

Great Barrier Reef
AUSTRALIA

The reef, which consists of around 2,500 individual reefs and 500 coral islands, stretches for more than 2,000 kilometres along the northeastern coast of Australia. Its "architects" are stony coral polyps, which live in symbiosis with blue-green algae. The larvae of the polyps, which are already capable of swimming, hatch in the spring and then settle in colonies on the reef near the water's surface while their skeletons form. After some time, they die and their calcareous tubes are ground into fine sand. The algae "bind" the sand into another reef layer, on which new young polyps can settle in the following year. Over millennia, the reefs and islands have grown in this way. Around 1,500 species of fish live in the waters surrounding the reef, and hundreds and thousands of bird, coral and mollusc species also call it home.

This unique underwater world is equally fascinating from above. When flying over the Great Barrier Reef, the reef shimmers in all shades of blue.

Eerily yet elegantly, the giant manta ray glides through the water. This fascinating creature, which can weigh up to two tonnes and reach a wingspan of up to seven metres, is always seen accompanied by its cleaning crew – cleaner fish scrub its gill rakes, which are used to filter food from the water (above).

LOCATION Along the coastline of the Great Barrier Reef, northeastern Australia

SIZE 8,934.53km^2

UNESCO World Heritage Site since 1988

Wet Tropics of Queensland
AUSTRALIA

This 9,000-square-kilometre area encompasses around 20 national parks as well as other protected regions. The tropical rainforest covers only parts of the mountain ridges of the Great Dividing Range, the valleys of the Great Escarpment and the coastal region of Queensland, where the tropical climate has remained stable for millions of years. This relatively undisturbed environment has allowed a rich diversity of animal and plant life to develop. Over 800 different tree species form a forest structured in several "layers". Beneath the light-blocking canopy of the towering trees, which reach up to 50 metres, more than 350 different higher plants grow, including ferns, orchids, mosses and lichens. About a third of all Australian marsupial and reptile species, as well as two-thirds of all bat and butterfly species, live in this comparatively small area.

The multi-coloured lorikeets (main picture) shine in the most beautiful rainbow colours. These adaptable parrots populate both rainforests and dry eucalyptus forests. In terms of colour, the Australian king parrot (bottom right) competes with the lorikeets, while the other inhabitants of the park, such as Boyd's forest dragon (above), adopt a more subdued colour scheme.

Right from top: Millaa Millaa Falls, green ringtail possum, red-legged pademelon and Australian king parrot.

LOCATION In the Alligator Rivers region, southeast of the city of Darwin

SIZE 19,804km²

ESTABLISHED 1981

UNESCO World Heritage Site since 1981

parksaustralia.gov.au/kakadu

Kakadu National Park
AUSTRALIA

Located approximately 170 kilometres southeast of Darwin, this national park covers around 20,000 square kilometres and encompasses five distinct landscape zones, and has been expanded several times. In the tidal areas of the rivers, the stilt roots of the mangroves are anchored in the mud, protecting the hinterland from the destructive effects of wave action. The coastal areas transform during the rainy season into a colourful carpet of lotus flowers, water lilies and floating ferns. Rare water birds, such as brolgas, jacanas, white-faced herons, black-necked storks and darters, are native here, as well as the saltwater crocodile, which can grow up to six metres in length. The adjacent uplands, with their diverse vegetation of open tropical forests, savannahs and grasslands, stretch across most of the park and provide refuge for endangered species such as dingoes and wallabies. Rare species of kangaroo live in the Arnhem Escarpment, a 500-kilometre-long cliff that runs from the southwest to the northeast of the park, as well as on the sandstone plateaus of Arnhem Land.

The park gained international fame in the mid-twentieth century when excavations uncovered stone tools dating back at least 30,000 years. Numerous rock paintings provide insight into the hunting habits, myths and customs of the Aboriginal tribes that lived here.

From Nourlangie Rock, (above) the view extends over the vast wetlands (opposite bottom).

The 150-metre-high Jim Jim Falls cascade into the Jim Jim plunge pool (opposite top and left).

LOCATION 440 kilometres south of Alice Springs
SIZE 1,325.5km²
ESTABLISHED 1987
UNESCO Biosphere Reserve since 1977
UNESCO World Heritage Site since 1977
parksaustralia.gov.au/uluru

Uluru-Kata Tjuta National Park
AUSTRALIA

In the heart of an extensive, barren dry savannah lies "the red heart of Australia", the Uluru-Kata Tjuta National Park. It is home to some of Australia's most famous natural wonders: the rocky inselberg Uluru (formerly known as Ayers Rock) and the 36 rock domes of Kata Tjuta, meaning "many heads". Its development, which began 570 million years ago, is closely linked to the formation of the Australian continent. The highly resilient rock of these formations weathered much more slowly than the surrounding rock masses, so today they stand as enormous, fossilized witnesses to the ancient past, rising from the plains. For over 10,000 years, the Anganu, an Aboriginal tribe, have lived here, believing their ancestors have always managed and cared for the land since the beginning of time.

Uluru

The heart of the national park is the majestic Uluru, which consists of a sandstone-like rock that shimmers in different shades of red depending on the time of day. Uluru is not only the geographical centre but also a mythical place for the Aboriginal people, with rock paintings and sacred sites. It is regarded as a meeting point of the ancestors, who, during their wanderings in the Dreamtime, created the land and all living things. The rock paintings on the outside of the rock tell the mythological story of how the land and the mountain were formed. According to the legend, it rose from the earth in a fierce battle between two groups from the Dreamtime, turning the spirits of the two combatants into stone. To this day, the mountain is sacred to the Aboriginal people, which is why since 2019, no one is allowed to climb Uluru.

The compact massif of Uluru looks especially impressive when viewed from the air (top).

At ground level, it is possible to see the forest that surrounds Uluru (bottom).

LOCATION Eastern shore of Lake Eyre, approximately 750 kilometres north of Adelaide
SIZE 13,592.51km^2
ESTABLISHED 1985
parks.sa.gov.au/parks/Kati-thanda-lake-eyre-national-park

Lake Eyre National Park
AUSTRALIA

Lake Eyre is the largest salt lake in Australia, the lowest point on the Australian continent, at 15 metres below sea level, and the centre of the Lake Eyre Basin. During the rainy season, the rivers bring water from the Outback. The amount of monsoonal rain determines how much water reaches the lake and how deep it becomes. About every three years, the water level reaches 1.5 metres. Since its discovery in 1841, the lake has only been completely filled with water three times. However, even after this rare event, the northern lake dries up again in the continental, hot, dry climate of South Australia. As the water evaporates, deposits of salt-rich clay remain, which over time accumulate into a thick layer. Edward John Eyre was the first white man to cross the Nullarbor Plain on foot from Fowler's Bay to what is now Albany, on a journey that took nearly three years to complete.

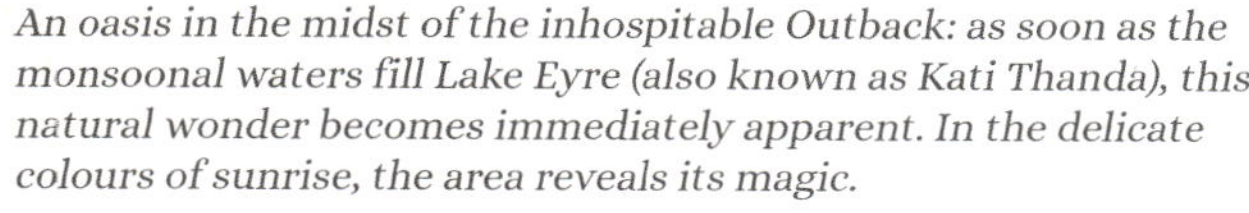

An oasis in the midst of the inhospitable Outback: as soon as the monsoonal waters fill Lake Eyre (also known as Kati Thanda), this natural wonder becomes immediately apparent. In the delicate colours of sunrise, the area reveals its magic.

LOCATION North Island: the national park stretches across the regions of Manawatu-Wanganui and Waikato, near Lake Taupo

SIZE 795.96km²

ESTABLISHED 1907

UNESCO World Heritage Site since 1990

Tongariro National Park
NEW ZEALAND

In 1887, Chief Te Heuheu Tukino gifted the land surrounding the Tongariro Volcano, which is sacred to the Maori, to the New Zealand government with the condition that it be protected for all people. The government acquired additional land and designated it as a national park in 1907. Since 1990, the area, which covers around 795 square kilometres, has been protected as a UNESCO World Heritage Site. The core of the park consists of three active volcanic systems: Tongariro (1,967 metres) is the closest to Lake Taupo. It is the smallest of the three volcanoes and gave the national park its name. To the south is Ngauruhoe (2,287 metres), the most active volcano in the park. The third, multi-coned volcano, Ruapehu, at 2,797 metres, is the highest peak on the North Island. Its summit stretches over three kilometres and features an acidic crater lake and six small glaciers.

The most memorable aspect of Tongariro National Park is not its relatively unremarkable scree slopes, but the rich colours of its lakes, craters and the sky above.

LOCATION Covers the entire southwest corner of the South Island, adjacent to Mount Aspiring National Park

SIZE 12,607km^2

ESTABLISHED 1952

UNESCO World Heritage Site since 1990

fiordland.org.nz

Fiordland National Park
NEW ZEALAND

The largest national park in New Zealand, covering around 12,520 square kilometres, is arguably the most beautiful in the country: snow-capped mountains form the backdrop, while vast beech forests with centuries-old, moss-covered trees, fill the foreground. Crystal-clear rivers and tranquil lakes fill broad valleys shaped by retreating glaciers. Here, you can find around 700 endemic plant species and several endangered animal species. Majestic fjords line the West Coast, of which only Milford Sound is accessible by road. This area is one of the most popular trekking destinations in the world. The experience is only slightly marred by the pesky black "sandflies" which, according to a Maori legend, were created by the goddess of death to prevent hikers from fully enjoying the beauty of the landscape.

The most beautiful end of the world? The steep, forested cliff faces of Milford Sound flow into the Tasman Sea. The road to Milford Sound is one of the most scenic mountain routes in the world. From Te Anau, it skirts a lake and then traverses largely untouched landscapes with magnificent viewpoints.

The curious kea (above) is one of the most intelligent birds in the world – a fact that helps it survive in the Southern Alps.

LOCATION Approximately 590 kilometres southeast of Stewart Island

SIZE 112.86km^2

UNESCO World Heritage Site since 1998

Campbell Island
NEW ZEALAND

Campbell Island is part of the Campbell Island group and lies about 700 kilometres south of New Zealand's mainland. The island, a remnant of a volcanic cone, is highly rugged. Inland, mountains rise, the highest being Mount Honey (558 metres). Fjords wind into the land on the eastern side of the island, while the western side is dominated by cliffs and steep coastlines. Throughout its colonial history, the island's nature was heavily exploited: seals and whales were hunted in the waters around Campbell Island, and in 1895 a pioneer established a farm on the island. Up to 8,000 sheep lived here, destroying many plant species. In recent decades, a monumental effort was made to remove the sheep, goats and pigs from the island, and poison was used to eradicate the rat population, allowing nature to recover.

Although Campbell Island's nature has had a difficult past and often had to defend itself against introduced species, the island now has a remarkably diverse flora and fauna, including rockhopper penguins (left) and southern elephant seals (above).

Opposite: this young southern elephant seal seems to be enjoying life. No wonder, considering his environment, which, after years of settlement, is slowly returning to its original state.

The Maori call the yellow-eyed penguins "hoiho", meaning "shouter". These extremely rare creatures tend to make a lot of noise, trumpeting loudly to draw attention to themselves (top left).

LOCATION Palau, south of Babeldaob, between Koror and Peleliu in the Pacific Ocean

SIZE 1,000km²

UNESCO World Heritage Site since 2012

Southern Lagoon of the Chelbacheb Islands
PALAU

A long dark shadow appears in the turquoise water, as large as a whale shark or an orca, yet it doesn't move. Upon closer inspection, it becomes clear that it is wearing a second skin made of coral. The first skin is made of rusted iron, for the shadow is none other than the wreck of a Japanese warplane. Such discoveries are common in the Palau Islands of the South Pacific. What might appear, from a distance, to be an image of paradise, has a turbulent history. During World War II, a fierce battle raged here between the Japanese and American forces, leaving behind not only aircraft wrecks but also rusty tanks, jeeps and bunkers on land. Apart from this, these roughly 300 uninhabited islands are popular with divers, as the underwater world has been able to flourish here, far from any human civilisation.

From above, the Chelbacheb Islands (or Rock Islands) look like moss-covered stones in the turquoise water. Here, illustrious marine creatures like pearl oysters (above) or damselfish (opposite) can be found.

LOCATION The Solomon Islands; east of Papua New Guinea, northeast of Australia and north of Vangunu Island in the Pacific Ocean
SIZE 700km²

Marovo Lagoon
SOLOMON ISLANDS

To the north, the Marovo Lagoon is bordered by New Georgia Island. To the south, Gatukai and Vangunu also mark the eastern boundary of the largest saltwater lagoon in the world. This natural gem is dotted with countless small islands. Underwater, the area teems with life. The polyps of the stony corals gently sway in the waves of the Pacific. Parrotfish and clownfish dart between the branches of their calcareous skeletons, while crustaceans, sponges and sea cucumbers make their home here. Inevitably, predators are also present, with swift reef sharks and majestically gliding rays making appearances. Life on land was much less idyllic until quite recently, however. The infamous Marovo Lagoon had long been feared due to the headhunters who lived there.

A squid eating a giant clam (above).
Small pictures (clockwise from top left): jellyfish, leopard grouper, hermit crab, red-spotted blenny, giant clam, bubbletip anemone, disc anemone and Pederson's cleaner shrimp.

LOCATION In the southern Pacific Ocean, northeast of Tahiti; part of the Tuamotu Archipelago in French Polynesia

SIZE 79km² (mainland), 1,600km² (lagoon)

Rangiroa
FRENCH POLYNESIA

The Tuamotu Archipelago consists of more than 70 atolls, arranged in a double chain about 1,500 kilometres long, scattered over a marine area roughly the size of Central Europe. The largest atoll spans over 1,500 square kilometres and is encircled by around 240 motus. Its name, "Rangiroa" can be loosely translated as "wide sky". Like most of the atolls in the archipelago, Rangiroa only rises a few metres above sea level. However, the lagoon offers exceptional opportunities to engage with the underwater world of the South Seas. You don't even need diving equipment to experience something extraordinary. In fact, harmless reef sharks are often found in the shallow waters near the dreamlike sandy beaches.

This is what one imagines a South Sea paradise to be: white sand, turquoise waters, blue skies and green palm trees. The islands of the Tuamotu Archipelago come very close to this ideal image.

The lagoon is full of life. While sharks tend to be solitary, the smaller fish live in large, protective schools.

LOCATION At the centre of the Society Islands, north of Tahiti, in the southern Pacific Ocean

SIZE 38km²

Lagoon of Bora Bora
FRENCH POLYNESIA

An aquamarine lagoon scattered with tiny islands, and the distinctive silhouette of a lush green mountain at its centre, creates a fairytale image. The volcano is half-submerged, which, when viewed from the air, lends the whole scene a mystical character. Bora Bora, located at the centre of the Society Islands, is only about 38 square kilometres in size. Around 7,500 inhabitants live in this paradise, whose ancient name, "Mai Te Pora", means "created by the gods". How fitting for such a dream destination. Revered as the "Pearl of the Pacific", Bora Bora is one of the most famous of the Society Islands. Its mountains rise like green turrets above the blue and turquoise waters of a lagoon, which is the remnant of a volcanic crater – as are the two hilly islets off the west coast. A long chain of sandy motus lines the reef to the north and east. From Vaitape, the island's main town, a steep path leads through forested slopes to Mount Pahia. The hike takes several hours and requires a good level of fitness – and a guide. However, local operators also offer island safaris here.

Whether the Dutchman Jacob Roggeveen visited Bora Bora during his circumnavigation of the world in 1722 is uncertain. What is clear, however, is that if he didn't, he missed out. James Cook, on the other hand, sighted the island in 1769, but was unable to land due to bad weather conditions. It wasn't until his third voyage in 1777 that he actually set foot on the island. What the explorers were denied back then is the aerial view. The atoll lies like a distinct triangle in the deep blue sea.

Photo credits

C = Corbis, G = Getty Images, M = Mauritius Images
Cover: Alexandre Seixas/Shutterstock.com (Zhangye National Park, China)
S. 4 Look/Andreas Strauß, S. 4 G/Anup Shah, S. 7 G/Peter Pinnock, S. 10/11 M/Alamy, S. 12 G/Peerakit JIrachetthakun, S. 12/13 G/Ramiro Torrents, S. 13 G/Gunnar Örn Árnason, S. 14/15 G/Subtik, S. 15 G/Arctic-Images, S. 16 G/Tunart, S. 16/17 G/Wei Hao Ho, S. 16/17 G/Southern Lightscapes-Australia, S. 16/17 G/Wei Hao Ho, S. 18/19 G/Wei Hao Ho, S. 18/19 G/Vvvita, S. 20 M/Willi Rolfes, S. 20 M/Stefan Huwiler, S. 20 M/Willi Rolfes, S. 20 M/Stefan Huwiler, S. 20/21 M/Ben Cranke, S. 22 G/Hans Strand, S. 22/23 G/Anders Ekholm, S. 22/23 G/Erlend Haarberg, S. 23 M/Erlend Haarberg, S. 23 G/Westend61, S. 23 G/Winfried Wisniewski, S. 23 M/Erlend Haarberg, S. 24/25 G/Marco Bottigelli, S. 25 iacomino FRiMAGES/Shutterstock.com, S. 26 M/Bernd Zoller, S. 26/27 M/Johan van der Wielen, S. 26/27 M/Jordi Bas Casas, S. 27 M/Philippe Clement, S. 27 M/Markus Varesvuo, S. 27 M/Jussi Murtosaari, S. 27 M/Reiner Bernhardt, S. 28/29 G/Mariuskasteckas, S. 29 G/Mariuskasteckas, S. 30 Amedeo lunco photographer/Shutterstock.com, S. 30/31 G/Pete Rowbottom, S. 32 G/Scott Robertson, S. 32/33 Look/robertharding, S. 32/33 M/Allan Wright, S. 33 G/Kathy Collins, S. 34 G/Eleanor Scriven, S. 34/35 G/John finney photography, S. 34/35 G/ChrisHepburn, S. 34/35 G/John finney photography, S. 35 M/Chris Herring, S. 36/37 G/James Osmond, S. 36/37 G/Antony Spencer Photography, S. 37 G/Mark Crocker - images through a lens, S. 38/39 G/MathieuRivrin, S. 40/41 G/Mario Colonel, S. 40/41 G/Paul Biris, S. 42/43 Richard Semik/Shutterstock.com, S. 43 G/Eric Rousset, S. 44/45 G/Rahan1991, S. 45 G/Bruno Donnangricchia, S. 46 G/Raimund Linke, S. 46/47 G/Daniel Bosma, S. 46/47 G/Andreas Kretschmer, S. 47 G/Westend61, S. 48/49 Look/Olafprotze, S. 49 Look/Tobias Richter, S. 50 M/Stefan Hefele, S. 50/51 G/Moritz Wolf, S. 50/51 G/DaitoZen, S. 52 G/Ketkarn sakultap, S. 52/53 M/Roberto Moiola, S. 54 G/Renelo, S. 54/55 G/Arto Hakola, S. 54/55 G/Sorin Rechitan, S. 55 G/Arto Hakola, S. 56 G/Michal Sleczek, S. 56/57 TTstudio/Shutterstock.com, S. 56/57 G/Karol Majewski, S. 57 G/Macroworld, S. 57 Kluciar Ivan/Shutterstock.com, S. 58 G/Alvaro Roxo, S. 58 G/Paulo Rocha, S. 58/59 G/FredConcha, S. 58/59 M/Roberto Moiola, S. 60/61 G/Marco Bottigelli, S. 60/61 G/Akrp, S. 61 G/Frank Lukasseck, S. 62 G/Julio López Saguar, S. 62/63 G/Jose Quintela, S. 64/65 M/Tilyo Rusev, S. 65 M/Mikel Bilbao Gorostiaga, S. 66 M/Alamy, S. 66 M/Ramon Navarro, S. 66 G/David Santiago Garcia, S. 66 G/Victor Ovies Arenas, S. 66/67 G/Cris Cantón Photography, S. 66/67 M/Bob Gibbons, S. 67 M/Loic Poidevin, S. 67 M/Roger Powell, S. 67 M/Ramon Navarro, S. 67 M/Ramon Navarro, S. 68/69 G/Frank Lukasseck, S. 68/69 G/Juan David Martin Ravelo, S. 69 G/Atlantide Phototravel, S. 70 G/Patryk_Kosmider, S. 70/71 G/Achim Thomae, S. 72/73 G/Michele D'Amico supersky77, S. 72/73 G/Stefady, S. 73 G/TroiseCarmineWashi www.flickr.com/photos/25517152@N05/, S. 74 G/Lorenzo Mattei, S. 74/75 G/Luigi Alesi, S. 74/75 G/Luigi Alesi, S. 76/77 G/Michele D'Amico supersky77, S. 77 G/Maxim K, S. 78/79 G/SimonSkafar, S. 79 Roxana Bashyrova/Shutterstock.com, S. 80 G/4FR, S. 80/81 G/Glcheng, S. 80/81 Mike Mareen/Shutterstock.com, S. 81 G/Romulic-Stojcic, S. 82 M/David Havel, S. 82/83 M/John Gooday, S. 82/83 RoStyle/Shutterstock.com, S. 84 G/Laurentiu-Mihai Panaete, S. 84/85 G/Marian Poar, S. 84/85 G/Istvan Kadar Photography, S. 85 G/Dragos Pop, S. 86 G/Maya Karkalicheva, S. 86 G/Maya Karkalicheva, S. 86/87 G/Maya Karkalicheva, S. 86/87 G/Maya Karkalicheva, S. 87 G/Maya Karkalicheva, S. 88/89 G/Carsten Schanter, S. 88/89 G/Evgeni Dinev Photography, S. 90/91 G/Anton Petrus, S. 91 G/Brian J. Skerry, S. 92/93 G/Manoj Shah, S. 94 M/robertharding, S. 94 M/Daniel Heuclin, S. 94 G/Kristian Bell, S. 94/95 G/Leonid Andronov, S. 94/95 M/Daniel Heuclin, S. 95 M/Alamy, S. 96 M/Thijs van den Burg, S. 96 M/Daniel Heuclin, S. 96/97 G/Ira Block, S. 97 M/Lesley van Loo, S. 97 M/Bruno Amicis, S. 98/99 M/Westend61, S. 99 G/Egmont Strigl, S. 100 G/Mansour Ali Photography, S. 100/101 M/Tom Till, S. 100/101 G/Cinoby, S. 102 Andrei Armiagov/Shutterstock.com, S. 102/103 G/Vincent Pommeyrol, S. 103 Gerald Robert Fischer/Shutterstock.com, S. 103 Levent Konuk/Shutterstock.com, S. 103 Kimmo Hagman/Shutterstock.com, S. 103 Dean1313/Shutterstock.com, S. 103 Kim_Briers/Shutterstock.com, S. 104 M/Michaela Walch, S. 104 G/John Elk, S. 104/105 G/Rudolf Ernst, S. 105 Ondrej Prosicky/Shutterstock.com, S. 105 G/Jeremy Woodhouse, S. 106 M/Ignacio Yufera, S. 106 M/Alamy, S. 106/107 M/Alamy, S. 106/107 G/BSIP, S. 107 M/Alamy, S. 107 G/BSIP, S. 108 G/ L. Romano, S. 108 M/Fiona Rogers, S. 108 M/Anup Shah, S. 108 M/Frans Lanting, S. 108/109 M/Robert Henno, S. 110/111 M/John Warburton-Lee, S. 111 M/SFM Titti Soldati, S. 112 G/Berndt Fischer, S. 112/113 M/Gerard Lacz, S. 112/113 G/R. Portolese , S. 112/113 G/Joel Sartore, S. 113 G/Martin Willis, S. 114 G/Laura M. Vear, S. 114/115 M/Matthias Graben, S. 116 M/Wim van den Heever, S. 116/117 M/Marg Wood, S. 116/117 G/Guenterguni, S. 117 Matt T Jackson/Shutterstock.com, S. 118 G/Joel Sartore, S. 118/119 M/Alamy, S. 118/119 G/Eric Baccega, S. 119 G/Jean-Paul Chatagnon, S. 119 M/Alamy, S. 120 G/Morgan Trimble, S. 120/121 G/Christopher Kidd, S. 120/121 Efimova Anna/Shutterstock.com, S. 121 M/Thomas Marent, S. 121 M/Nigel Pavitt, S. 121 feathercollector/Shutterstock.com, S. 121 Monika Hrdinova/Shutterstock.com, S. 122/123 G/Ignacio Palacios, S. 122/123 G/Feargus Cooney, S. 123 Look/Minden Pictures, S. 124 G/Miguel Sanz, S. 124/125 G/Vlapaev, S. 124/125 G/SoopySue, S. 125 G/Martin Harvey, S. 126/127 Aboubakar Malipula/Shutterstock.com, S. 127 G/1001slide, S. 128 G/Traumlichtfabrik, S. 128 G/Michael Nalley, S. 128 G/David Chen, S. 128/129 G/Jamie Friedland, S. 128/129 G/Mahtab Karimi, S. 129 G/Michael Poliza, S. 130/131 G/Bruce Alexander, S. 130/131 Alamy/Danita Delimont, S. 130/131 G/Russell Burden, S. 131 G/Guenterguni, S. 132 Look/Andreas Strauß, S. 132/133 Look/age fotostock, S. 132/133 Look/age fotostock, S. 133 G/Photography Aubrey Stoll, S. 134 G/Pol Rebaque, S. 134 G/Arctic-Images, S. 134/135 G/Buena Vista Images, S. 134/135 Ger Metselaar/Shutterstock.com, S. 136/137 G/Luis Davilla, S. 137 Dietmar Temps/Shutterstock.com, S. 138 NickEvansKZN/Shutterstock.com, S. 138/139 G/David McCormick, S. 138/139 G/Jason Grunstra, S. 139 M/Richard Du Toit, S. 140 M/David Noton Photography, S. 140/141 Lukas Bischoff Photograph/Shutterstock.com, S. 140/141 G/Emil von Maltitz, S. 142 G/Heinrich van den Berg, S. 142 G/Robert Harding Picture Libr. Ltd, S. 142 M/Pete Oxford, S. 142/143 G/Petri Oeschger, S. 142/143 G/James Hager, S. 143 G/Gunter Lenz, S. 144/145 M/Alamy, S. 144/145 M/Gillian Lloyd, S. 145 M/Alamy, S. 146 G/VW Pics, S. 146 G/VW Pics, S. 146 G/Chris Schmid, S. 146/147 M/Richard Du Toit, S. 147 G/Martin Harvey, S. 148 G/inusuke, S. 148/149 G/Sakis Papadopoulos, S. 150/151 Look/Rainer Mirau, S. 150/151 M/United Archives, S. 151 G/Rainer Mirau, S. 152/153 G/Infografick, S. 153 G/SPANI Arnaud, S. 154/155 G/Michele Falzone, S. 156 G/Nick Fitzhardinge, S. 156 M/robertharding, S. 156/157 G/Deddeda, S. 157 M/Alamy, S. 158/159 G/Darwin Wiggett, S. 159 M/Fotofeeling, S. 160/161 G/Damien Verrier, S. 161 M/Malcolm Schuyl, S. 161 M/Guy Runco, S. 162 G/Tom Walker, S. 162 M/Patrick Endres, S. 162/163 Look/Design Pics, S. 163 G/Jacob W. Frank, S. 163 G/Lijuan Guo Photography, S. 164 G/Donald M. Jones, S. 164 Menno Schaefer/Shutterstock.com, S. 164 G/Danita Delimont, S. 164 G/Spondylolithesis, S. 164 G/Matthias Breiter, S. 164 G/Don Johnston, S. 164/165 Look/Danita Delimont , S. 164/165 G/Yajnesh Bhat, S. 166 G/Peterlakomy, S. 166 M/Ben Barden, S. 166 G/Ben Pipe, S. 166/167 G/Alan Copson, S. 167 sumikophoto/Shutterstock.com, S. 167 G/JoSon, S. 168 G/James Forsyth, S. 168/169 G/Ignacio Palacios, S. 169 M/Alessandra Sarti, S. 169 G/Ignacio Palacios, S. 169 M/robertharding, S. 170 Ralf Broskvar/Shutterstock.com, S. 170 G/Alan W Cole, S. 170/171 G/Patrick Morris, S. 171 G/Witold Skrypczak, S. 171 M/Michael Weber, S. 171 G/Muha04, S. 172 G/Southern Lightscapes-Australia, S. 172/173 M/Rainer Mirau, S. 174/175 G/Dean Fikar, S. 175 Kyle Kephart/Shutterstock.com, S. 176 G/www.sierralara.com, S. 176/177 G/Franckreporter, S. 176/177 G/Keith Ladzinski, S. 177 G/Rich Reid, S. 178 G/PhotoviewPlus, S. 178/179 G/Tambako the Jaguar, S. 178/179 G/Justin Reznick Photography, S. 178/179 G/Tetra Images, S. 179 G/Diana Robinson Photography, S. 179 M/Ingo Arndt, S. 180/181 G/Art Wolfe, S. 181 G/Kevin Thrash, S. 182/183 M/Donald M. Jones, S. 183 M/Cristovao Oliveira, S. 184/185 M/Brusini AurÉlien, S. 185 G/Eyewave, S. 186 G/Richard Nowitz, S. 186 M/Christian Ziegler, S. 186/187 G/Pascal Moulinier, S. 186/187 G/Danita Delimont, S. 187 G/Andrew M. Snyder, S. 187 G/Andrew M. Snyder, S. 187 G/Tier Und Naturfotografie J und C Sohns, S. 187 G/Andrew M. Snyder, S. 187 L-N/Shutterstock.com, S. 188 G/Kryssia Campos, S. 188/189 M/Francesco Puntiroli, S. 189 Michal Sarauer/Shutterstock.com, S. 189 G/Javier Fernández Sánchez, S. 190 G/Jane Sweeney, S. 191 Holger Hennern/Shutterstock.com, S. 191 Caio Pederneiras/Shutterstock.com, S. 191 G/Edson Vandeira, S. 191 G/Edson Vandeira, S. 192 G/Andrea Pistolesi, S. 192/193 M/Pete Oxford, S. 194 M/Bjanka Kadic, S. 194 M/Luciano Candisani, S. 194 G/Pintai Suchachaisri, S. 194/195 G/Tirc83, S. 195 M/Jacques Jangoux, S. 195 M/Zena Elea, S. 195 M/Tui De Roy, S. 195 M/Zena Elea, S. 196 G/Gabrielle Therin-Weise, S. 196 M/Frederic Soreau, S. 196 G/Westend61, S. 196/197 M/Andre Seale, S. 196/197 G/Pierronimo, S. 196/197 G/Guido Agüero, S. 197 Alejo Miranda/Shutterstock.com, S. 197 SATRIA NANGISAN/Shutterstock.com, S. 197 Joe McDonald/Shutterstock.com, S. 197 Anna Kucherova/Shutterstock.com, S. 198 G/Alex Saberi, S. 198/199 G/Alex Saberi, S. 198/199 G/Jesse Kraft, S. 198/199 G/Gerard Blignaut, S. 199 M/Gerald Abele, S. 200 M/Tui De Roy, S. 200 G/Joel Sartore, S. 200 G/I love nature! - I love Brazil!, S. 200 G/Todd Gipstein, S. 200/201 G/Westend61, S. 200/201 G/Giovani Cordioli, S. 200/201 G/James R.D. Scott, S. 201 MightyPix/Shutterstock.com, S. 202/203 M/Wei Hao Ho, S. 203 G/Jmichel Deborde, S. 204 M/Chris Stenger, S. 204/205 G/Mariusz Kluzniak, S. 204/205 G/Martinelli73, S. 204/205 G/Marco Bittel, S. 205 G/Juergen Ritterbach, S. 206 G/Gabriel Sperandio, S. 206/207 G/Agustavop, S. 206/207 G/Massimo Borchi, S. 207 G/Aumphotography, S. 208 G/Bruce Hood, S. 208/209 G/Eric Hanson, S. 208/209 G/Gcoles, S. 210 G/Philippe Widling, S. 210/211 G/Klaus Balzano, S. 210/211 G/Mariusz Kluzniak, S. 212 Look/age fotostock, S. 212/213 G/Global_Pics, S. 214 G/Ruben Earth, S. 214/215 G/MB Photography, S. 214/215 G/Andy Rouse, S. 215 G/Arthur Machado, S. 216/217 G/ViewStock, S. 218 G/Denis Svechnikov, S. 218 M/Julien Garcia, S. 218 G/Denis Svechnikov, S. 218/219 M/Martin Lindsay, S. 219 G/Denis Svechnikov, S. 220/221 G/Anna Dobos, S. 220/221 G/Danny Hu , S. 221 G/Reimar Gaertner, S. 222/223 G/Ilan Shacham, S. 222/223 G/Ilan Shacham, S. 222/223 G/Ido Meirovich, S. 223 G/Ilan Shacham, S. 224 G/Anton Petrus, S. 224/225 G/CNicholas Olesen, S. 224/225 G/Boom Chuthai, S. 225 G/Wanson Luk, S. 226 M/Alamy, S. 226 G/Jean-Philippe Tournut, S. 226 G/@ Didier Marti, S. 226/227 G/Ratnakorn Piyasirisorost, S. 227 G/Jean-Philippe Tournut, S. 228 G/Francesco Vaninetti Photo, S. 228/229 G/Anton Petrus, S. 228/229 G/SinghaphanAllB, S. 229 G/Anton Petrus, S. 230/231 G/Yuhan Liao, S. 230/231 G/Feng Wei Photography, S. 232 G/Kelly Cheng, S. 232 G/Kelly Cheng, S. 232 M/Sam Yue, S. 232/233 G/ViewStock, S. 234/235 G/Aphotostory, S. 235 G/Istvan Kadar Photography, S. 236 G/MelindaChan, S. 236/237 G/Kittisun kittayacharoenpong, S. 236/237 G/Haibo Bl, S. 238 godi photo/Shutterstock.com, S. 238/239 G/Topic Photo Agency, S. 238/239 G/wtsoki905, S. 239 M/Joe Blossom, S. 239 G/Jong-Won Heo, S. 240 G/Sunrise@dawn Photography, S. 240/241 G/CJFAN, S. 240/241 G/FuYi Chen, S. 241 G/Mr Monchai Awae, S. 241 G/FLPA/John Holmes, S. 241 G/FuYi Chen, S. 242/243 G/Yuga Kurita, S. 243 G/I love Photo and Apple., S. 244 G/Tomosang, S. 244 M/John Steele, S. 244/245 G/Putt Sakdhnagool, S. 245 G/imagenavi, S. 246 G/Asifsaeed313, S. 246/247 G/Punnawit Suwuttananun, S. 248 G/Punnawit Suwuttananun, S. 248/249 G/Feng Wei Photography, S. 250 G/Giulio Mignani, S. 250 G/Image Work/amanaimagesRF, S. 250/251 G/Jacek Kadaj, S. 250/251 M/Danita Delimont, S. 251 M/Gerard Lacz, S. 252 G/February, S. 252/253 M/Eric Dragesco, S. 252/253 G/David Davidov, S. 253 G/Athit Perawongmetha, S. 254/255 G/Steve Winter, S. 254/255 G/© Neha & Chittaranjan Desai, S. 255 G/Wolfgang Kaehler, S. 256 G/Steve Winter, S. 256/257 G/Saranga Deva De Alwis, S. 256/257 M/Westend61, S. 256/257 G/Kanwal Sandhu, S. 257 G/Daniele Carotenuto Photography, S. 257 M/Ashish & Shanthi Chandola, S. 258 G/Kwanchai_k photograph, S. 258/259 G/Anuchit kamsongmueang, S. 258/259 G/Nobythai, S. 259 G/www.tonnaja.com, S. 260 G/Stephen Frink, S. 260/261 G/Kampee patisena, S. 260/261 G/Steve De Neef, S. 261 G/Takau99, S. 261 G/Chanon Kanjanavasoontara, S. 261 Rich Carey/Shutterstock.com, S. 261 Gerald Robert Fischer/Shutterstock.com, S. 262 G/Damocean, S. 262/263 G/Bento Fotography, S. 262/263 G/Dollia Sheombar, S. 264/265 G/Ho Ngoc Binh, S. 264/265 G/Chi My. Trung Hamaru. Vietnam., S. 265 G/Ho Ngoc Binh, S. 266/267 G/Kat Clay, S. 267 G/Jonas Ginter, S. 268 G/Fletcher & BAYLIS, S. 268/269 G/Phil Curtis, S. 268/269 G/Tristan Savatier, S. 269 G/Juhku, S. 270 M/Alamy, S. 270 M/Alamy, S. 270 M/Alamy, S. 270 M/Alamy, S. 270 M/Alamy, S. 270 M/Alamy, S. 271 M/David Santiago Garcia, S. 271 M/Alamy, S. 271 M/Alamy, S. 271 M/Alamy, S. 272 M/Florian Neukirchen, S. 272/273 G/Puripat Lertpunyaroj, S. 272/273 G/Dinno Sandoval, S. 274 M/Anup Shah, S. 274 G/C. DANI I. JESKE, S. 274 M/Anup Shah, S. 274 M/Anup Shah, S. 274/275 M/Alamy, S. 276/277 G/Supoj Buranaprapapong, S. 276/277 G/Raung Binaia, S. 277 G/Aumphotography, S. 278/279 Look/Rainer Mirau, S. 280/281 G/Mevans, S. 281 G/Haveseen, S. 282 M/Konrad Wothe, S. 282 M/Martin Willis, S. 282 yoko van de geyn/Shutterstock.com, S. 282 M/Martin Willis, S. 282/283 M/Konrad Wothe, S. 283 G/Jaykayl, S. 284 Janelle Lugge/Shutterstock.com, S. 284 Look/Karl Johaentges, S. 284/285 iacomino FRiMAGES/Shutterstock.com, S. 285 Daniela Constantinescu/Shutterstock.com, S. 286/287 G/Ignacio Palacios, S. 286/287 G/Paul A. Souders, S. 288/289 G/Julie Fletcher, S. 289 G/Theo Allofs, S. 290 G/Matteo Colombo, S. 290/291 C/Mario Cipriani, S. 290/291 G/Piskunov, S. 291 G/Sino Images, S. 292 M/Andy Trowbridge, S. 292/293 G/irmaferreira, S. 292/293 G/Chiara Salvadori, S. 294 M/Tui De Roy, S. 294 M/Ingrid Visser, S. 294/295 Giedriius/Shutterstock.com, S. 294/295 M/Tui De Roy, S. 295 M/David Osborn , S. 296 G/Ethan Daniels/Stocktrek Images, S. 296/297 G/Tan Yilmaz, S. 296/297 Oscar Olsson/Shutterstock.com, S. 297 G/By wildestanimal, S. 298 M/Chris Newbert, S. 298 Elliotte Rusty Harold/Shutterstock.com, S. 298 NaturePicsFilms/Shutterstock.com, S. 298/298 G/Peter Pinnock, S. 298/298 G/Hal Beral, S. 298/298 Christophe Rouziou/Shutterstock.com, S. 299 scubaluna/Shutterstock.com, S. 299 Vojce/Shutterstock.com, S. 299 M/Norbert Wu, S. 299 M/Chris Newbert, S. 300/301 G/Mlenny, S. 301 Damsea/Shutterstock.com, S. 302/303 G/Premium, S. 303 G/Dahlquist Ron.

Originally published as *Wilde Erde*

www.kunth-verlag.de
English edition published by APA Publications under exclusive agreement with Kunth Verlag Mairdumont GmbH & Co. KG

ISBN 9781835294017
1st English edition 2025

Printed in China

Editor: Rachel Lawrence
Head of Publishing: Sarah Clark
Publishing Technology Manager: Rebeka Davies
Authors: Özlem Ahmetoglu, Stephanie Fischer, Katinka Holupirek, Michaela Jancauskas, Laura Joppien, Andrea Lammert, Andrea Rudolf